Painter's Palette

Fairhaven
Media

FAIRHAVEN MEDIA

Painter's Palette
Copyright 2020 © by Hubert and Sheila Robertson

Cover design and Interior Layout: Sheila Robertson
Cover artwork: Hubert Robertson

Printed in the United States of America

ISBN: 978-1-947729-07-0
Business Records, Professional Painting

Painter's Palette

We started painting in 1985 and we would love to have a record book of all the tens of thousands of gallons of paint that we have applied since then. But more than a record book for the amount of paint, we wish we had a record of all the people we've painted for through the years. We've worked for some great people and we've also had our share of doozies!

This book helps with both kinds of customers. Some people you just want to help because you like them. Some people you need the record for your own protection and peace of mind.

No matter why you use *Painter's Palette*, we hope that it will prove to be an invaluable tool to you in the coming years. Having a detailed record of each job has been a very good thing for our business and we trust it will be for yours also.

Date _____

Job Name _____ ph # _____

Job Address _____

Paint Brand _____

Room Name _____

Wall Color _____
- ☐ Flat   ☐ Satin
- ☐ Matte   ☐ Semi gloss
- ☐ Eggshell   ☐ High gloss

Ceiling Color _____
- ☐ Flat   ☐ Satin
- ☐ Matte   ☐ Semi gloss
- ☐ Eggshell   ☐ High gloss

Trim Color _____
- ☐ Flat   ☐ Satin
- ☐ Matte   ☐ Semi gloss
- ☐ Eggshell   ☐ High gloss

Notes

Room Name _____

Wall Color _____
- ☐ Flat   ☐ Satin
- ☐ Matte   ☐ Semi gloss
- ☐ Eggshell   ☐ High gloss

Ceiling Color _____
- ☐ Flat   ☐ Satin
- ☐ Matte   ☐ Semi gloss
- ☐ Eggshell   ☐ High gloss

Trim Color _____
- ☐ Flat   ☐ Satin
- ☐ Matte   ☐ Semi gloss
- ☐ Eggshell   ☐ High gloss

Notes

Date

Job Name   ph #

Job Address

Paint Brand

Room Name

	□ Flat	□ Satin
Wall Color	□ Matte	□ Semi gloss
	□ Eggshell	□ High gloss
	□ Flat	□ Satin
Ceiling Color	□ Matte	□ Semi gloss
	□ Eggshell	□ High gloss
	□ Flat	□ Satin
Trim Color	□ Matte	□ Semi gloss
	□ Eggshell	□ High gloss

Notes

Room Name

	□ Flat	□ Satin
Wall Color	□ Matte	□ Semi gloss
	□ Eggshell	□ High gloss
	□ Flat	□ Satin
Ceiling Color	□ Matte	□ Semi gloss
	□ Eggshell	□ High gloss
	□ Flat	□ Satin
Trim Color	□ Matte	□ Semi gloss
	□ Eggshell	□ High gloss

Notes

Date _____

Job Name _____ ph # _____

Job Address _____

Paint Brand _____

Room Name _____

Wall Color _____
- ☐ Flat   ☐ Satin
- ☐ Matte   ☐ Semi gloss
- ☐ Eggshell   ☐ High gloss

Ceiling Color _____
- ☐ Flat   ☐ Satin
- ☐ Matte   ☐ Semi gloss
- ☐ Eggshell   ☐ High gloss

Trim Color _____
- ☐ Flat   ☐ Satin
- ☐ Matte   ☐ Semi gloss
- ☐ Eggshell   ☐ High gloss

Notes

Room Name _____

Wall Color _____
- ☐ Flat   ☐ Satin
- ☐ Matte   ☐ Semi gloss
- ☐ Eggshell   ☐ High gloss

Ceiling Color _____
- ☐ Flat   ☐ Satin
- ☐ Matte   ☐ Semi gloss
- ☐ Eggshell   ☐ High gloss

Trim Color _____
- ☐ Flat   ☐ Satin
- ☐ Matte   ☐ Semi gloss
- ☐ Eggshell   ☐ High gloss

Notes

Date _____

Job Name _____ ph # _____

Job Address _____

Paint Brand _____

Room Name _____

Wall Color _____
- ☐ Flat ☐ Satin
- ☐ Matte ☐ Semi gloss
- ☐ Eggshell ☐ High gloss

Ceiling Color _____
- ☐ Flat ☐ Satin
- ☐ Matte ☐ Semi gloss
- ☐ Eggshell ☐ High gloss

Trim Color _____
- ☐ Flat ☐ Satin
- ☐ Matte ☐ Semi gloss
- ☐ Eggshell ☐ High gloss

Notes

Room Name _____

Wall Color _____
- ☐ Flat ☐ Satin
- ☐ Matte ☐ Semi gloss
- ☐ Eggshell ☐ High gloss

Ceiling Color _____
- ☐ Flat ☐ Satin
- ☐ Matte ☐ Semi gloss
- ☐ Eggshell ☐ High gloss

Trim Color _____
- ☐ Flat ☐ Satin
- ☐ Matte ☐ Semi gloss
- ☐ Eggshell ☐ High gloss

Notes

Date _____

Job Name _____ ph # _____

Job Address _____

Paint Brand _____

Room Name

Wall Color _____	☐ Flat ☐ Matte ☐ Eggshell	☐ Satin ☐ Semi gloss ☐ High gloss
Ceiling Color _____	☐ Flat ☐ Matte ☐ Eggshell	☐ Satin ☐ Semi gloss ☐ High gloss
Trim Color _____	☐ Flat ☐ Matte ☐ Eggshell	☐ Satin ☐ Semi gloss ☐ High gloss

Notes

Room Name

Wall Color _____	☐ Flat ☐ Matte ☐ Eggshell	☐ Satin ☐ Semi gloss ☐ High gloss
Ceiling Color _____	☐ Flat ☐ Matte ☐ Eggshell	☐ Satin ☐ Semi gloss ☐ High gloss
Trim Color _____	☐ Flat ☐ Matte ☐ Eggshell	☐ Satin ☐ Semi gloss ☐ High gloss

Notes

Date _____

Job Name _____ ph # _____

Job Address _____

Paint Brand _____

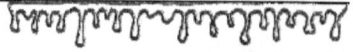

Room Name _____

Wall Color _____	☐ Flat ☐ Matte ☐ Eggshell	☐ Satin ☐ Semi gloss ☐ High gloss
Ceiling Color _____	☐ Flat ☐ Matte ☐ Eggshell	☐ Satin ☐ Semi gloss ☐ High gloss
Trim Color _____	☐ Flat ☐ Matte ☐ Eggshell	☐ Satin ☐ Semi gloss ☐ High gloss

Notes

Room Name _____

Wall Color _____	☐ Flat ☐ Matte ☐ Eggshell	☐ Satin ☐ Semi gloss ☐ High gloss
Ceiling Color _____	☐ Flat ☐ Matte ☐ Eggshell	☐ Satin ☐ Semi gloss ☐ High gloss
Trim Color _____	☐ Flat ☐ Matte ☐ Eggshell	☐ Satin ☐ Semi gloss ☐ High gloss

Notes

Date _____

Job Name _____ ph # _____

Job Address _____

Paint Brand _____

Room Name _____

Wall Color _____
- ☐ Flat ☐ Satin
- ☐ Matte ☐ Semi gloss
- ☐ Eggshell ☐ High gloss

Ceiling Color _____
- ☐ Flat ☐ Satin
- ☐ Matte ☐ Semi gloss
- ☐ Eggshell ☐ High gloss

Trim Color _____
- ☐ Flat ☐ Satin
- ☐ Matte ☐ Semi gloss
- ☐ Eggshell ☐ High gloss

Notes

Room Name _____

Wall Color _____
- ☐ Flat ☐ Satin
- ☐ Matte ☐ Semi gloss
- ☐ Eggshell ☐ High gloss

Ceiling Color _____
- ☐ Flat ☐ Satin
- ☐ Matte ☐ Semi gloss
- ☐ Eggshell ☐ High gloss

Trim Color _____
- ☐ Flat ☐ Satin
- ☐ Matte ☐ Semi gloss
- ☐ Eggshell ☐ High gloss

Notes

Date _____

Job Name _____ ph # _____

Job Address _____

Paint Brand _____

Room Name _____

Wall Color _____
- [ ] Flat   [ ] Satin
- [ ] Matte   [ ] Semi gloss
- [ ] Eggshell [ ] High gloss

Ceiling Color _____
- [ ] Flat   [ ] Satin
- [ ] Matte   [ ] Semi gloss
- [ ] Eggshell [ ] High gloss

Trim Color _____
- [ ] Flat   [ ] Satin
- [ ] Matte   [ ] Semi gloss
- [ ] Eggshell [ ] High gloss

Notes

Room Name _____

Wall Color _____
- [ ] Flat   [ ] Satin
- [ ] Matte   [ ] Semi gloss
- [ ] Eggshell [ ] High gloss

Ceiling Color _____
- [ ] Flat   [ ] Satin
- [ ] Matte   [ ] Semi gloss
- [ ] Eggshell [ ] High gloss

Trim Color _____
- [ ] Flat   [ ] Satin
- [ ] Matte   [ ] Semi gloss
- [ ] Eggshell [ ] High gloss

Notes

Date _____

Job Name _____ ph # _____

Job Address _____

Paint Brand _____

Room Name

Wall Color _____
- [ ] Flat　　[ ] Satin
- [ ] Matte　[ ] Semi gloss
- [ ] Eggshell [ ] High gloss

Ceiling Color _____
- [ ] Flat　　[ ] Satin
- [ ] Matte　[ ] Semi gloss
- [ ] Eggshell [ ] High gloss

Trim Color _____
- [ ] Flat　　[ ] Satin
- [ ] Matte　[ ] Semi gloss
- [ ] Eggshell [ ] High gloss

Notes

Room Name

Wall Color _____
- [ ] Flat　　[ ] Satin
- [ ] Matte　[ ] Semi gloss
- [ ] Eggshell [ ] High gloss

Ceiling Color _____
- [ ] Flat　　[ ] Satin
- [ ] Matte　[ ] Semi gloss
- [ ] Eggshell [ ] High gloss

Trim Color _____
- [ ] Flat　　[ ] Satin
- [ ] Matte　[ ] Semi gloss
- [ ] Eggshell [ ] High gloss

Notes

Date _____

Job Name _____ ph # _____

Job Address _____

Paint Brand _____

Room Name

Wall Color _____

☐ Flat   ☐ Satin
☐ Matte   ☐ Semi gloss
☐ Eggshell   ☐ High gloss

Ceiling Color _____

☐ Flat   ☐ Satin
☐ Matte   ☐ Semi gloss
☐ Eggshell   ☐ High gloss

Trim Color _____

☐ Flat   ☐ Satin
☐ Matte   ☐ Semi gloss
☐ Eggshell   ☐ High gloss

Notes

Room Name

Wall Color _____

☐ Flat   ☐ Satin
☐ Matte   ☐ Semi gloss
☐ Eggshell   ☐ High gloss

Ceiling Color _____

☐ Flat   ☐ Satin
☐ Matte   ☐ Semi gloss
☐ Eggshell   ☐ High gloss

Trim Color _____

☐ Flat   ☐ Satin
☐ Matte   ☐ Semi gloss
☐ Eggshell   ☐ High gloss

Notes

Date _____

Job Name _____ ph # _____

Job Address _____

Paint Brand _____

Room Name _____

Wall Color _____
- ☐ Flat ☐ Satin
- ☐ Matte ☐ Semi gloss
- ☐ Eggshell ☐ High gloss

Ceiling Color _____
- ☐ Flat ☐ Satin
- ☐ Matte ☐ Semi gloss
- ☐ Eggshell ☐ High gloss

Trim Color _____
- ☐ Flat ☐ Satin
- ☐ Matte ☐ Semi gloss
- ☐ Eggshell ☐ High gloss

Notes

Room Name _____

Wall Color _____
- ☐ Flat ☐ Satin
- ☐ Matte ☐ Semi gloss
- ☐ Eggshell ☐ High gloss

Ceiling Color _____
- ☐ Flat ☐ Satin
- ☐ Matte ☐ Semi gloss
- ☐ Eggshell ☐ High gloss

Trim Color _____
- ☐ Flat ☐ Satin
- ☐ Matte ☐ Semi gloss
- ☐ Eggshell ☐ High gloss

Notes

Date _____

Job Name _____ ph # _____

Job Address _____

Paint Brand _____

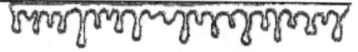

Room Name _____

Wall Color _____
- [ ] Flat [ ] Satin
- [ ] Matte [ ] Semi gloss
- [ ] Eggshell [ ] High gloss

Ceiling Color _____
- [ ] Flat [ ] Satin
- [ ] Matte [ ] Semi gloss
- [ ] Eggshell [ ] High gloss

Trim Color _____
- [ ] Flat [ ] Satin
- [ ] Matte [ ] Semi gloss
- [ ] Eggshell [ ] High gloss

Notes

Room Name _____

Wall Color _____
- [ ] Flat [ ] Satin
- [ ] Matte [ ] Semi gloss
- [ ] Eggshell [ ] High gloss

Ceiling Color _____
- [ ] Flat [ ] Satin
- [ ] Matte [ ] Semi gloss
- [ ] Eggshell [ ] High gloss

Trim Color _____
- [ ] Flat [ ] Satin
- [ ] Matte [ ] Semi gloss
- [ ] Eggshell [ ] High gloss

Notes

Date _____

Job Name _____ ph # _____

Job Address _____

Paint Brand _____

Room Name _____

Wall Color _____
- ☐ Flat ☐ Satin
- ☐ Matte ☐ Semi gloss
- ☐ Eggshell ☐ High gloss

Ceiling Color _____
- ☐ Flat ☐ Satin
- ☐ Matte ☐ Semi gloss
- ☐ Eggshell ☐ High gloss

Trim Color _____
- ☐ Flat ☐ Satin
- ☐ Matte ☐ Semi gloss
- ☐ Eggshell ☐ High gloss

Notes

Room Name _____

Wall Color _____
- ☐ Flat ☐ Satin
- ☐ Matte ☐ Semi gloss
- ☐ Eggshell ☐ High gloss

Ceiling Color _____
- ☐ Flat ☐ Satin
- ☐ Matte ☐ Semi gloss
- ☐ Eggshell ☐ High gloss

Trim Color _____
- ☐ Flat ☐ Satin
- ☐ Matte ☐ Semi gloss
- ☐ Eggshell ☐ High gloss

Notes

Date

Job Name   ph #

Job Address

Paint Brand

Room Name

	☐ Flat ☐ Satin
Wall Color	☐ Matte ☐ Semi gloss
	☐ Eggshell ☐ High gloss
	☐ Flat ☐ Satin
Ceiling Color	☐ Matte ☐ Semi gloss
	☐ Eggshell ☐ High gloss
	☐ Flat ☐ Satin
Trim Color	☐ Matte ☐ Semi gloss
	☐ Eggshell ☐ High gloss

Notes

Room Name

	☐ Flat ☐ Satin
Wall Color	☐ Matte ☐ Semi gloss
	☐ Eggshell ☐ High gloss
	☐ Flat ☐ Satin
Ceiling Color	☐ Matte ☐ Semi gloss
	☐ Eggshell ☐ High gloss
	☐ Flat ☐ Satin
Trim Color	☐ Matte ☐ Semi gloss
	☐ Eggshell ☐ High gloss

Notes

Date _____

Job Name _____ ph # _____

Job Address _____

Paint Brand _____

Room Name _____

Wall Color _____
☐ Flat	☐ Satin
☐ Matte	☐ Semi gloss
☐ Eggshell	☐ High gloss

Ceiling Color _____
☐ Flat	☐ Satin
☐ Matte	☐ Semi gloss
☐ Eggshell	☐ High gloss

Trim Color _____
☐ Flat	☐ Satin
☐ Matte	☐ Semi gloss
☐ Eggshell	☐ High gloss

Notes

Room Name _____

Wall Color _____
☐ Flat	☐ Satin
☐ Matte	☐ Semi gloss
☐ Eggshell	☐ High gloss

Ceiling Color _____
☐ Flat	☐ Satin
☐ Matte	☐ Semi gloss
☐ Eggshell	☐ High gloss

Trim Color _____
☐ Flat	☐ Satin
☐ Matte	☐ Semi gloss
☐ Eggshell	☐ High gloss

Notes

Date _____

Job Name _____ ph # _____

Job Address _____

Paint Brand _____

Room Name _____

Wall Color _____

☐ Flat		☐ Satin	
☐ Matte		☐ Semi gloss	
☐ Eggshell		☐ High gloss	

Ceiling Color _____

☐ Flat		☐ Satin	
☐ Matte		☐ Semi gloss	
☐ Eggshell		☐ High gloss	

Trim Color _____

☐ Flat		☐ Satin	
☐ Matte		☐ Semi gloss	
☐ Eggshell		☐ High gloss	

Notes

Room Name _____

Wall Color _____

☐ Flat		☐ Satin	
☐ Matte		☐ Semi gloss	
☐ Eggshell		☐ High gloss	

Ceiling Color _____

☐ Flat		☐ Satin	
☐ Matte		☐ Semi gloss	
☐ Eggshell		☐ High gloss	

Trim Color _____

☐ Flat		☐ Satin	
☐ Matte		☐ Semi gloss	
☐ Eggshell		☐ High gloss	

Notes

Date _____

Job Name _____ ph # _____

Job Address _____

Paint Brand _____

Room Name _____

Wall Color _____
- ☐ Flat ☐ Satin
- ☐ Matte ☐ Semi gloss
- ☐ Eggshell ☐ High gloss

Ceiling Color _____
- ☐ Flat ☐ Satin
- ☐ Matte ☐ Semi gloss
- ☐ Eggshell ☐ High gloss

Trim Color _____
- ☐ Flat ☐ Satin
- ☐ Matte ☐ Semi gloss
- ☐ Eggshell ☐ High gloss

Notes

Room Name _____

Wall Color _____
- ☐ Flat ☐ Satin
- ☐ Matte ☐ Semi gloss
- ☐ Eggshell ☐ High gloss

Ceiling Color _____
- ☐ Flat ☐ Satin
- ☐ Matte ☐ Semi gloss
- ☐ Eggshell ☐ High gloss

Trim Color _____
- ☐ Flat ☐ Satin
- ☐ Matte ☐ Semi gloss
- ☐ Eggshell ☐ High gloss

Notes

Date _____

Job Name _____   ph # _____

Job Address _____

Paint Brand _____

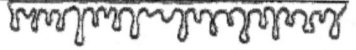

Room Name _____

Wall Color _____
☐ Flat ☐ Satin
☐ Matte ☐ Semi gloss
☐ Eggshell ☐ High gloss

Ceiling Color _____
☐ Flat ☐ Satin
☐ Matte ☐ Semi gloss
☐ Eggshell ☐ High gloss

Trim Color _____
☐ Flat ☐ Satin
☐ Matte ☐ Semi gloss
☐ Eggshell ☐ High gloss

Notes

Room Name _____

Wall Color _____
☐ Flat ☐ Satin
☐ Matte ☐ Semi gloss
☐ Eggshell ☐ High gloss

Ceiling Color _____
☐ Flat ☐ Satin
☐ Matte ☐ Semi gloss
☐ Eggshell ☐ High gloss

Trim Color _____
☐ Flat ☐ Satin
☐ Matte ☐ Semi gloss
☐ Eggshell ☐ High gloss

Notes

Date _____

Job Name _____ ph # _____

Job Address _____

Paint Brand _____

Room Name _____

☐ Flat	☐ Satin
☐ Matte	☐ Semi gloss
☐ Eggshell	☐ High gloss

Wall Color _____

☐ Flat	☐ Satin
☐ Matte	☐ Semi gloss
☐ Eggshell	☐ High gloss

Ceiling Color _____

☐ Flat	☐ Satin
☐ Matte	☐ Semi gloss
☐ Eggshell	☐ High gloss

Trim Color _____

Notes

Room Name _____

☐ Flat	☐ Satin
☐ Matte	☐ Semi gloss
☐ Eggshell	☐ High gloss

Wall Color _____

☐ Flat	☐ Satin
☐ Matte	☐ Semi gloss
☐ Eggshell	☐ High gloss

Ceiling Color _____

☐ Flat	☐ Satin
☐ Matte	☐ Semi gloss
☐ Eggshell	☐ High gloss

Trim Color _____

Notes

Date _____

Job Name _____ ph # _____

Job Address _____

Paint Brand _____

Room Name _____

Wall Color _____
- ☐ Flat ☐ Satin
- ☐ Matte ☐ Semi gloss
- ☐ Eggshell ☐ High gloss

Ceiling Color _____
- ☐ Flat ☐ Satin
- ☐ Matte ☐ Semi gloss
- ☐ Eggshell ☐ High gloss

Trim Color _____
- ☐ Flat ☐ Satin
- ☐ Matte ☐ Semi gloss
- ☐ Eggshell ☐ High gloss

Notes

Room Name _____

Wall Color _____
- ☐ Flat ☐ Satin
- ☐ Matte ☐ Semi gloss
- ☐ Eggshell ☐ High gloss

Ceiling Color _____
- ☐ Flat ☐ Satin
- ☐ Matte ☐ Semi gloss
- ☐ Eggshell ☐ High gloss

Trim Color _____
- ☐ Flat ☐ Satin
- ☐ Matte ☐ Semi gloss
- ☐ Eggshell ☐ High gloss

Notes

Date _____

Job Name _____ ph # _____

Job Address _____

Paint Brand _____

Room Name _____

☐ Flat	☐ Satin
☐ Matte	☐ Semi gloss
☐ Eggshell	☐ High gloss

Wall Color _____

☐ Flat	☐ Satin
☐ Matte	☐ Semi gloss
☐ Eggshell	☐ High gloss

Ceiling Color _____

☐ Flat	☐ Satin
☐ Matte	☐ Semi gloss
☐ Eggshell	☐ High gloss

Trim Color _____

Notes

Room Name _____

☐ Flat	☐ Satin
☐ Matte	☐ Semi gloss
☐ Eggshell	☐ High gloss

Wall Color _____

☐ Flat	☐ Satin
☐ Matte	☐ Semi gloss
☐ Eggshell	☐ High gloss

Ceiling Color _____

☐ Flat	☐ Satin
☐ Matte	☐ Semi gloss
☐ Eggshell	☐ High gloss

Trim Color _____

Notes

Date _____

Job Name _____ ph # _____

Job Address _____

Paint Brand _____

Room Name

Wall Color _____

- [ ] Flat
- [ ] Matte
- [ ] Eggshell
- [ ] Satin
- [ ] Semi gloss
- [ ] High gloss

Ceiling Color _____

- [ ] Flat
- [ ] Matte
- [ ] Eggshell
- [ ] Satin
- [ ] Semi gloss
- [ ] High gloss

Trim Color _____

- [ ] Flat
- [ ] Matte
- [ ] Eggshell
- [ ] Satin
- [ ] Semi gloss
- [ ] High gloss

Notes

Room Name

Wall Color _____

- [ ] Flat
- [ ] Matte
- [ ] Eggshell
- [ ] Satin
- [ ] Semi gloss
- [ ] High gloss

Ceiling Color _____

- [ ] Flat
- [ ] Matte
- [ ] Eggshell
- [ ] Satin
- [ ] Semi gloss
- [ ] High gloss

Trim Color _____

- [ ] Flat
- [ ] Matte
- [ ] Eggshell
- [ ] Satin
- [ ] Semi gloss
- [ ] High gloss

Notes

Date _____

Job Name _____ ph # _____

Job Address _____

Paint Brand _____

Room Name
_____

☐ Flat	☐ Satin
☐ Matte	☐ Semi gloss
☐ Eggshell	☐ High gloss

Wall Color _____

☐ Flat	☐ Satin
☐ Matte	☐ Semi gloss
☐ Eggshell	☐ High gloss

Ceiling Color _____

☐ Flat	☐ Satin
☐ Matte	☐ Semi gloss
☐ Eggshell	☐ High gloss

Trim Color _____

Notes

Room Name
_____

☐ Flat	☐ Satin
☐ Matte	☐ Semi gloss
☐ Eggshell	☐ High gloss

Wall Color _____

☐ Flat	☐ Satin
☐ Matte	☐ Semi gloss
☐ Eggshell	☐ High gloss

Ceiling Color _____

☐ Flat	☐ Satin
☐ Matte	☐ Semi gloss
☐ Eggshell	☐ High gloss

Trim Color _____

Notes

Date _____

Job Name _____   ph # _____

Job Address _____

Paint Brand _____

Room Name

Wall Color _____
- ☐ Flat ☐ Satin
- ☐ Matte ☐ Semi gloss
- ☐ Eggshell ☐ High gloss

Ceiling Color _____
- ☐ Flat ☐ Satin
- ☐ Matte ☐ Semi gloss
- ☐ Eggshell ☐ High gloss

Trim Color _____
- ☐ Flat ☐ Satin
- ☐ Matte ☐ Semi gloss
- ☐ Eggshell ☐ High gloss

Notes

Room Name

Wall Color _____
- ☐ Flat ☐ Satin
- ☐ Matte ☐ Semi gloss
- ☐ Eggshell ☐ High gloss

Ceiling Color _____
- ☐ Flat ☐ Satin
- ☐ Matte ☐ Semi gloss
- ☐ Eggshell ☐ High gloss

Trim Color _____
- ☐ Flat ☐ Satin
- ☐ Matte ☐ Semi gloss
- ☐ Eggshell ☐ High gloss

Notes

Date _____

Job Name _____ ph # _____

Job Address _____

Paint Brand _____

Room Name _____

Wall Color _____
- ☐ Flat ☐ Satin
- ☐ Matte ☐ Semi gloss
- ☐ Eggshell ☐ High gloss

Ceiling Color _____
- ☐ Flat ☐ Satin
- ☐ Matte ☐ Semi gloss
- ☐ Eggshell ☐ High gloss

Trim Color _____
- ☐ Flat ☐ Satin
- ☐ Matte ☐ Semi gloss
- ☐ Eggshell ☐ High gloss

Notes

Room Name _____

Wall Color _____
- ☐ Flat ☐ Satin
- ☐ Matte ☐ Semi gloss
- ☐ Eggshell ☐ High gloss

Ceiling Color _____
- ☐ Flat ☐ Satin
- ☐ Matte ☐ Semi gloss
- ☐ Eggshell ☐ High gloss

Trim Color _____
- ☐ Flat ☐ Satin
- ☐ Matte ☐ Semi gloss
- ☐ Eggshell ☐ High gloss

Notes

Date _____

Job Name _____   ph # _____

Job Address _____

Paint Brand _____

Room Name _____

Wall Color _____
- ☐ Flat ☐ Satin
- ☐ Matte ☐ Semi gloss
- ☐ Eggshell ☐ High gloss

Ceiling Color _____
- ☐ Flat ☐ Satin
- ☐ Matte ☐ Semi gloss
- ☐ Eggshell ☐ High gloss

Trim Color _____
- ☐ Flat ☐ Satin
- ☐ Matte ☐ Semi gloss
- ☐ Eggshell ☐ High gloss

Notes

Room Name _____

Wall Color _____
- ☐ Flat ☐ Satin
- ☐ Matte ☐ Semi gloss
- ☐ Eggshell ☐ High gloss

Ceiling Color _____
- ☐ Flat ☐ Satin
- ☐ Matte ☐ Semi gloss
- ☐ Eggshell ☐ High gloss

Trim Color _____
- ☐ Flat ☐ Satin
- ☐ Matte ☐ Semi gloss
- ☐ Eggshell ☐ High gloss

Notes

Date _____

Job Name _____ ph # _____

Job Address _____

Paint Brand _____

Room Name
_____

☐ Flat	☐ Satin
☐ Matte	☐ Semi gloss
☐ Eggshell	☐ High gloss

Wall Color _____

☐ Flat	☐ Satin
☐ Matte	☐ Semi gloss
☐ Eggshell	☐ High gloss

Ceiling Color _____

☐ Flat	☐ Satin
☐ Matte	☐ Semi gloss
☐ Eggshell	☐ High gloss

Trim Color _____

Notes

Room Name
_____

☐ Flat	☐ Satin
☐ Matte	☐ Semi gloss
☐ Eggshell	☐ High gloss

Wall Color _____

☐ Flat	☐ Satin
☐ Matte	☐ Semi gloss
☐ Eggshell	☐ High gloss

Ceiling Color _____

☐ Flat	☐ Satin
☐ Matte	☐ Semi gloss
☐ Eggshell	☐ High gloss

Trim Color _____

Notes

Date _____

Job Name _____   ph # _____

Job Address _____

Paint Brand _____

Room Name _____

Wall Color _____
- [ ] Flat
- [ ] Matte
- [ ] Eggshell
- [ ] Satin
- [ ] Semi gloss
- [ ] High gloss

Ceiling Color _____
- [ ] Flat
- [ ] Matte
- [ ] Eggshell
- [ ] Satin
- [ ] Semi gloss
- [ ] High gloss

Trim Color _____
- [ ] Flat
- [ ] Matte
- [ ] Eggshell
- [ ] Satin
- [ ] Semi gloss
- [ ] High gloss

Notes

Room Name _____

Wall Color _____
- [ ] Flat
- [ ] Matte
- [ ] Eggshell
- [ ] Satin
- [ ] Semi gloss
- [ ] High gloss

Ceiling Color _____
- [ ] Flat
- [ ] Matte
- [ ] Eggshell
- [ ] Satin
- [ ] Semi gloss
- [ ] High gloss

Trim Color _____
- [ ] Flat
- [ ] Matte
- [ ] Eggshell
- [ ] Satin
- [ ] Semi gloss
- [ ] High gloss

Notes

Date _____

Job Name _____ ph # _____

Job Address _____

Paint Brand _____

Room Name _____

Wall Color _____

☐ Flat	☐ Satin
☐ Matte	☐ Semi gloss
☐ Eggshell	☐ High gloss

Ceiling Color _____

☐ Flat	☐ Satin
☐ Matte	☐ Semi gloss
☐ Eggshell	☐ High gloss

Trim Color _____

☐ Flat	☐ Satin
☐ Matte	☐ Semi gloss
☐ Eggshell	☐ High gloss

Notes

Room Name _____

Wall Color _____

☐ Flat	☐ Satin
☐ Matte	☐ Semi gloss
☐ Eggshell	☐ High gloss

Ceiling Color _____

☐ Flat	☐ Satin
☐ Matte	☐ Semi gloss
☐ Eggshell	☐ High gloss

Trim Color _____

☐ Flat	☐ Satin
☐ Matte	☐ Semi gloss
☐ Eggshell	☐ High gloss

Notes

Date _____

Job Name _____ ph # _____

Job Address _____

Paint Brand _____
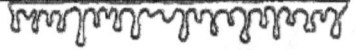

Room Name _____

Wall Color _____
- ☐ Flat ☐ Satin
- ☐ Matte ☐ Semi gloss
- ☐ Eggshell ☐ High gloss

Ceiling Color _____
- ☐ Flat ☐ Satin
- ☐ Matte ☐ Semi gloss
- ☐ Eggshell ☐ High gloss

Trim Color _____
- ☐ Flat ☐ Satin
- ☐ Matte ☐ Semi gloss
- ☐ Eggshell ☐ High gloss

Notes

Room Name _____

Wall Color _____
- ☐ Flat ☐ Satin
- ☐ Matte ☐ Semi gloss
- ☐ Eggshell ☐ High gloss

Ceiling Color _____
- ☐ Flat ☐ Satin
- ☐ Matte ☐ Semi gloss
- ☐ Eggshell ☐ High gloss

Trim Color _____
- ☐ Flat ☐ Satin
- ☐ Matte ☐ Semi gloss
- ☐ Eggshell ☐ High gloss

Notes

Date _____

Job Name _____ ph # _____

Job Address _____

Paint Brand _____

Room Name
_____

Wall Color _____
☐ Flat ☐ Satin
☐ Matte ☐ Semi gloss
☐ Eggshell ☐ High gloss

Ceiling Color _____
☐ Flat ☐ Satin
☐ Matte ☐ Semi gloss
☐ Eggshell ☐ High gloss

Trim Color _____
☐ Flat ☐ Satin
☐ Matte ☐ Semi gloss
☐ Eggshell ☐ High gloss

Notes

Room Name
_____

Wall Color _____
☐ Flat ☐ Satin
☐ Matte ☐ Semi gloss
☐ Eggshell ☐ High gloss

Ceiling Color _____
☐ Flat ☐ Satin
☐ Matte ☐ Semi gloss
☐ Eggshell ☐ High gloss

Trim Color _____
☐ Flat ☐ Satin
☐ Matte ☐ Semi gloss
☐ Eggshell ☐ High gloss

Notes

Date _____

Job Name _____   ph # _____

Job Address _____

Paint Brand _____

Room Name _____

Wall Color _____
- [ ] Flat
- [ ] Matte
- [ ] Eggshell
- [ ] Satin
- [ ] Semi gloss
- [ ] High gloss

Ceiling Color _____
- [ ] Flat
- [ ] Matte
- [ ] Eggshell
- [ ] Satin
- [ ] Semi gloss
- [ ] High gloss

Trim Color _____
- [ ] Flat
- [ ] Matte
- [ ] Eggshell
- [ ] Satin
- [ ] Semi gloss
- [ ] High gloss

Notes

Room Name _____

Wall Color _____
- [ ] Flat
- [ ] Matte
- [ ] Eggshell
- [ ] Satin
- [ ] Semi gloss
- [ ] High gloss

Ceiling Color _____
- [ ] Flat
- [ ] Matte
- [ ] Eggshell
- [ ] Satin
- [ ] Semi gloss
- [ ] High gloss

Trim Color _____
- [ ] Flat
- [ ] Matte
- [ ] Eggshell
- [ ] Satin
- [ ] Semi gloss
- [ ] High gloss

Notes

Date _____

Job Name _____   ph # _____

Job Address _____

Paint Brand _____

Room Name _____

Wall Color _____	☐ Flat ☐ Matte ☐ Eggshell	☐ Satin ☐ Semi gloss ☐ High gloss	
Ceiling Color _____	☐ Flat ☐ Matte ☐ Eggshell	☐ Satin ☐ Semi gloss ☐ High gloss	
Trim Color _____	☐ Flat ☐ Matte ☐ Eggshell	☐ Satin ☐ Semi gloss ☐ High gloss	

Notes

Room Name _____

Wall Color _____	☐ Flat ☐ Matte ☐ Eggshell	☐ Satin ☐ Semi gloss ☐ High gloss	
Ceiling Color _____	☐ Flat ☐ Matte ☐ Eggshell	☐ Satin ☐ Semi gloss ☐ High gloss	
Trim Color _____	☐ Flat ☐ Matte ☐ Eggshell	☐ Satin ☐ Semi gloss ☐ High gloss	

Notes

Date _____

Job Name _____ ph # _____

Job Address _____

Paint Brand _____

Room Name

Wall Color
- [ ] Flat   [ ] Satin
- [ ] Matte [ ] Semi gloss
- [ ] Eggshell [ ] High gloss

Ceiling Color
- [ ] Flat   [ ] Satin
- [ ] Matte [ ] Semi gloss
- [ ] Eggshell [ ] High gloss

Trim Color
- [ ] Flat   [ ] Satin
- [ ] Matte [ ] Semi gloss
- [ ] Eggshell [ ] High gloss

Notes

Room Name

Wall Color
- [ ] Flat   [ ] Satin
- [ ] Matte [ ] Semi gloss
- [ ] Eggshell [ ] High gloss

Ceiling Color
- [ ] Flat   [ ] Satin
- [ ] Matte [ ] Semi gloss
- [ ] Eggshell [ ] High gloss

Trim Color
- [ ] Flat   [ ] Satin
- [ ] Matte [ ] Semi gloss
- [ ] Eggshell [ ] High gloss

Notes

Date _____

Job Name _____ ph # _____

Job Address _____

Paint Brand _____

Room Name _____

Wall Color _____

- ☐ Flat ☐ Satin
- ☐ Matte ☐ Semi gloss
- ☐ Eggshell ☐ High gloss

Ceiling Color _____

- ☐ Flat ☐ Satin
- ☐ Matte ☐ Semi gloss
- ☐ Eggshell ☐ High gloss

Trim Color _____

- ☐ Flat ☐ Satin
- ☐ Matte ☐ Semi gloss
- ☐ Eggshell ☐ High gloss

Notes

Room Name _____

Wall Color _____

- ☐ Flat ☐ Satin
- ☐ Matte ☐ Semi gloss
- ☐ Eggshell ☐ High gloss

Ceiling Color _____

- ☐ Flat ☐ Satin
- ☐ Matte ☐ Semi gloss
- ☐ Eggshell ☐ High gloss

Trim Color _____

- ☐ Flat ☐ Satin
- ☐ Matte ☐ Semi gloss
- ☐ Eggshell ☐ High gloss

Notes

Date _____

Job Name _____ ph # _____

Job Address _____

Paint Brand _____

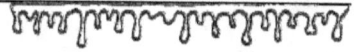

Room Name _____

Wall Color _____
- ☐ Flat   ☐ Satin
- ☐ Matte   ☐ Semi gloss
- ☐ Eggshell ☐ High gloss

Ceiling Color _____
- ☐ Flat   ☐ Satin
- ☐ Matte   ☐ Semi gloss
- ☐ Eggshell ☐ High gloss

Trim Color _____
- ☐ Flat   ☐ Satin
- ☐ Matte   ☐ Semi gloss
- ☐ Eggshell ☐ High gloss

Notes

Room Name _____

Wall Color _____
- ☐ Flat   ☐ Satin
- ☐ Matte   ☐ Semi gloss
- ☐ Eggshell ☐ High gloss

Ceiling Color _____
- ☐ Flat   ☐ Satin
- ☐ Matte   ☐ Semi gloss
- ☐ Eggshell ☐ High gloss

Trim Color _____
- ☐ Flat   ☐ Satin
- ☐ Matte   ☐ Semi gloss
- ☐ Eggshell ☐ High gloss

Notes

Date _____

Job Name _____ ph # _____

Job Address _____

Paint Brand _____

Room Name _____

Wall Color _____

☐ Flat ☐ Satin
☐ Matte ☐ Semi gloss
☐ Eggshell ☐ High gloss

Ceiling Color _____

☐ Flat ☐ Satin
☐ Matte ☐ Semi gloss
☐ Eggshell ☐ High gloss

Trim Color _____

☐ Flat ☐ Satin
☐ Matte ☐ Semi gloss
☐ Eggshell ☐ High gloss

Notes

Room Name _____

Wall Color _____

☐ Flat ☐ Satin
☐ Matte ☐ Semi gloss
☐ Eggshell ☐ High gloss

Ceiling Color _____

☐ Flat ☐ Satin
☐ Matte ☐ Semi gloss
☐ Eggshell ☐ High gloss

Trim Color _____

☐ Flat ☐ Satin
☐ Matte ☐ Semi gloss
☐ Eggshell ☐ High gloss

Notes

41

Date _____

Job Name _____ ph # _____

Job Address _____

Paint Brand _____

Room Name

Wall Color _____
- ☐ Flat   ☐ Satin
- ☐ Matte   ☐ Semi gloss
- ☐ Eggshell   ☐ High gloss

Ceiling Color _____
- ☐ Flat   ☐ Satin
- ☐ Matte   ☐ Semi gloss
- ☐ Eggshell   ☐ High gloss

Trim Color _____
- ☐ Flat   ☐ Satin
- ☐ Matte   ☐ Semi gloss
- ☐ Eggshell   ☐ High gloss

Notes

Room Name

Wall Color _____
- ☐ Flat   ☐ Satin
- ☐ Matte   ☐ Semi gloss
- ☐ Eggshell   ☐ High gloss

Ceiling Color _____
- ☐ Flat   ☐ Satin
- ☐ Matte   ☐ Semi gloss
- ☐ Eggshell   ☐ High gloss

Trim Color _____
- ☐ Flat   ☐ Satin
- ☐ Matte   ☐ Semi gloss
- ☐ Eggshell   ☐ High gloss

Notes

Date _____

Job Name _____   ph # _____

Job Address _____

Paint Brand _____

Room Name
_____

Wall Color _____
- ☐ Flat ☐ Satin
- ☐ Matte ☐ Semi gloss
- ☐ Eggshell ☐ High gloss

Ceiling Color _____
- ☐ Flat ☐ Satin
- ☐ Matte ☐ Semi gloss
- ☐ Eggshell ☐ High gloss

Trim Color _____
- ☐ Flat ☐ Satin
- ☐ Matte ☐ Semi gloss
- ☐ Eggshell ☐ High gloss

Notes

Room Name
_____

Wall Color _____
- ☐ Flat ☐ Satin
- ☐ Matte ☐ Semi gloss
- ☐ Eggshell ☐ High gloss

Ceiling Color _____
- ☐ Flat ☐ Satin
- ☐ Matte ☐ Semi gloss
- ☐ Eggshell ☐ High gloss

Trim Color _____
- ☐ Flat ☐ Satin
- ☐ Matte ☐ Semi gloss
- ☐ Eggshell ☐ High gloss

Notes

Date _____

Job Name _____ ph # _____

Job Address _____

Paint Brand _____

Room Name _____

Wall Color _____
- [ ] Flat [ ] Satin
- [ ] Matte [ ] Semi gloss
- [ ] Eggshell [ ] High gloss

Ceiling Color _____
- [ ] Flat [ ] Satin
- [ ] Matte [ ] Semi gloss
- [ ] Eggshell [ ] High gloss

Trim Color _____
- [ ] Flat [ ] Satin
- [ ] Matte [ ] Semi gloss
- [ ] Eggshell [ ] High gloss

Notes

Room Name _____

Wall Color _____
- [ ] Flat [ ] Satin
- [ ] Matte [ ] Semi gloss
- [ ] Eggshell [ ] High gloss

Ceiling Color _____
- [ ] Flat [ ] Satin
- [ ] Matte [ ] Semi gloss
- [ ] Eggshell [ ] High gloss

Trim Color _____
- [ ] Flat [ ] Satin
- [ ] Matte [ ] Semi gloss
- [ ] Eggshell [ ] High gloss

Notes

Date _____

Job Name _____ ph # _____

Job Address _____

Paint Brand _____

Room Name

Wall Color _____
☐ Flat ☐ Satin
☐ Matte ☐ Semi gloss
☐ Eggshell ☐ High gloss

Ceiling Color _____
☐ Flat ☐ Satin
☐ Matte ☐ Semi gloss
☐ Eggshell ☐ High gloss

Trim Color _____
☐ Flat ☐ Satin
☐ Matte ☐ Semi gloss
☐ Eggshell ☐ High gloss

Notes

Room Name

Wall Color _____
☐ Flat ☐ Satin
☐ Matte ☐ Semi gloss
☐ Eggshell ☐ High gloss

Ceiling Color _____
☐ Flat ☐ Satin
☐ Matte ☐ Semi gloss
☐ Eggshell ☐ High gloss

Trim Color _____
☐ Flat ☐ Satin
☐ Matte ☐ Semi gloss
☐ Eggshell ☐ High gloss

Notes

Date _____

Job Name _____ ph # _____

Job Address _____

Paint Brand _____

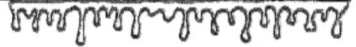

Room Name _____

Wall Color _____

- [ ] Flat
- [ ] Matte
- [ ] Eggshell
- [ ] Satin
- [ ] Semi gloss
- [ ] High gloss

Ceiling Color _____

- [ ] Flat
- [ ] Matte
- [ ] Eggshell
- [ ] Satin
- [ ] Semi gloss
- [ ] High gloss

Trim Color _____

- [ ] Flat
- [ ] Matte
- [ ] Eggshell
- [ ] Satin
- [ ] Semi gloss
- [ ] High gloss

Notes

Room Name _____

Wall Color _____

- [ ] Flat
- [ ] Matte
- [ ] Eggshell
- [ ] Satin
- [ ] Semi gloss
- [ ] High gloss

Ceiling Color _____

- [ ] Flat
- [ ] Matte
- [ ] Eggshell
- [ ] Satin
- [ ] Semi gloss
- [ ] High gloss

Trim Color _____

- [ ] Flat
- [ ] Matte
- [ ] Eggshell
- [ ] Satin
- [ ] Semi gloss
- [ ] High gloss

Notes

Date _____

Job Name _____ ph # _____

Job Address _____

Paint Brand _____

Room Name

Wall Color _____
- ☐ Flat ☐ Satin
- ☐ Matte ☐ Semi gloss
- ☐ Eggshell ☐ High gloss

Ceiling Color _____
- ☐ Flat ☐ Satin
- ☐ Matte ☐ Semi gloss
- ☐ Eggshell ☐ High gloss

Trim Color _____
- ☐ Flat ☐ Satin
- ☐ Matte ☐ Semi gloss
- ☐ Eggshell ☐ High gloss

Notes

Room Name

Wall Color _____
- ☐ Flat ☐ Satin
- ☐ Matte ☐ Semi gloss
- ☐ Eggshell ☐ High gloss

Ceiling Color _____
- ☐ Flat ☐ Satin
- ☐ Matte ☐ Semi gloss
- ☐ Eggshell ☐ High gloss

Trim Color _____
- ☐ Flat ☐ Satin
- ☐ Matte ☐ Semi gloss
- ☐ Eggshell ☐ High gloss

Notes

Date _____

Job Name _____ ph # _____

Job Address _____

Paint Brand _____

Room Name _____

Wall Color _____
- [ ] Flat
- [ ] Matte
- [ ] Eggshell
- [ ] Satin
- [ ] Semi gloss
- [ ] High gloss

Ceiling Color _____
- [ ] Flat
- [ ] Matte
- [ ] Eggshell
- [ ] Satin
- [ ] Semi gloss
- [ ] High gloss

Trim Color _____
- [ ] Flat
- [ ] Matte
- [ ] Eggshell
- [ ] Satin
- [ ] Semi gloss
- [ ] High gloss

Notes

Room Name _____

Wall Color _____
- [ ] Flat
- [ ] Matte
- [ ] Eggshell
- [ ] Satin
- [ ] Semi gloss
- [ ] High gloss

Ceiling Color _____
- [ ] Flat
- [ ] Matte
- [ ] Eggshell
- [ ] Satin
- [ ] Semi gloss
- [ ] High gloss

Trim Color _____
- [ ] Flat
- [ ] Matte
- [ ] Eggshell
- [ ] Satin
- [ ] Semi gloss
- [ ] High gloss

Notes

Date _____

Job Name _____ ph # _____

Job Address _____

Paint Brand _____

Room Name

Wall Color _____
- ☐ Flat ☐ Satin
- ☐ Matte ☐ Semi gloss
- ☐ Eggshell ☐ High gloss

Ceiling Color _____
- ☐ Flat ☐ Satin
- ☐ Matte ☐ Semi gloss
- ☐ Eggshell ☐ High gloss

Trim Color _____
- ☐ Flat ☐ Satin
- ☐ Matte ☐ Semi gloss
- ☐ Eggshell ☐ High gloss

Notes

Room Name

Wall Color _____
- ☐ Flat ☐ Satin
- ☐ Matte ☐ Semi gloss
- ☐ Eggshell ☐ High gloss

Ceiling Color _____
- ☐ Flat ☐ Satin
- ☐ Matte ☐ Semi gloss
- ☐ Eggshell ☐ High gloss

Trim Color _____
- ☐ Flat ☐ Satin
- ☐ Matte ☐ Semi gloss
- ☐ Eggshell ☐ High gloss

Notes

Date _____

Job Name _____ ph # _____

Job Address _____

Paint Brand _____

Room Name _____

Wall Color _____
- [ ] Flat
- [ ] Matte
- [ ] Eggshell
- [ ] Satin
- [ ] Semi gloss
- [ ] High gloss

Ceiling Color _____
- [ ] Flat
- [ ] Matte
- [ ] Eggshell
- [ ] Satin
- [ ] Semi gloss
- [ ] High gloss

Trim Color _____
- [ ] Flat
- [ ] Matte
- [ ] Eggshell
- [ ] Satin
- [ ] Semi gloss
- [ ] High gloss

Notes

Room Name _____

Wall Color _____
- [ ] Flat
- [ ] Matte
- [ ] Eggshell
- [ ] Satin
- [ ] Semi gloss
- [ ] High gloss

Ceiling Color _____
- [ ] Flat
- [ ] Matte
- [ ] Eggshell
- [ ] Satin
- [ ] Semi gloss
- [ ] High gloss

Trim Color _____
- [ ] Flat
- [ ] Matte
- [ ] Eggshell
- [ ] Satin
- [ ] Semi gloss
- [ ] High gloss

Notes

Date _____

Job Name _____ ph # _____

Job Address _____

Paint Brand _____

Room Name
_____

Wall Color _____

☐ Flat   ☐ Satin
☐ Matte   ☐ Semi gloss
☐ Eggshell   ☐ High gloss

Ceiling Color _____

☐ Flat   ☐ Satin
☐ Matte   ☐ Semi gloss
☐ Eggshell   ☐ High gloss

Trim Color _____

☐ Flat   ☐ Satin
☐ Matte   ☐ Semi gloss
☐ Eggshell   ☐ High gloss

Notes

Room Name
_____

Wall Color _____

☐ Flat   ☐ Satin
☐ Matte   ☐ Semi gloss
☐ Eggshell   ☐ High gloss

Ceiling Color _____

☐ Flat   ☐ Satin
☐ Matte   ☐ Semi gloss
☐ Eggshell   ☐ High gloss

Trim Color _____

☐ Flat   ☐ Satin
☐ Matte   ☐ Semi gloss
☐ Eggshell   ☐ High gloss

Notes

Date _____

Job Name _____ ph # _____

Job Address _____

Paint Brand _____

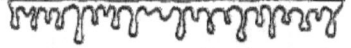

Room Name _____

Wall Color _____
☐ Flat ☐ Satin
☐ Matte ☐ Semi gloss
☐ Eggshell ☐ High gloss

Ceiling Color _____
☐ Flat ☐ Satin
☐ Matte ☐ Semi gloss
☐ Eggshell ☐ High gloss

Trim Color _____
☐ Flat ☐ Satin
☐ Matte ☐ Semi gloss
☐ Eggshell ☐ High gloss

Notes

Room Name _____

Wall Color _____
☐ Flat ☐ Satin
☐ Matte ☐ Semi gloss
☐ Eggshell ☐ High gloss

Ceiling Color _____
☐ Flat ☐ Satin
☐ Matte ☐ Semi gloss
☐ Eggshell ☐ High gloss

Trim Color _____
☐ Flat ☐ Satin
☐ Matte ☐ Semi gloss
☐ Eggshell ☐ High gloss

Notes

Date _____

Job Name _____ ph # _____

Job Address _____

Paint Brand _____

Room Name _____

Wall Color _____
- ☐ Flat ☐ Satin
- ☐ Matte ☐ Semi gloss
- ☐ Eggshell ☐ High gloss

Ceiling Color _____
- ☐ Flat ☐ Satin
- ☐ Matte ☐ Semi gloss
- ☐ Eggshell ☐ High gloss

Trim Color _____
- ☐ Flat ☐ Satin
- ☐ Matte ☐ Semi gloss
- ☐ Eggshell ☐ High gloss

Notes

Room Name _____

Wall Color _____
- ☐ Flat ☐ Satin
- ☐ Matte ☐ Semi gloss
- ☐ Eggshell ☐ High gloss

Ceiling Color _____
- ☐ Flat ☐ Satin
- ☐ Matte ☐ Semi gloss
- ☐ Eggshell ☐ High gloss

Trim Color _____
- ☐ Flat ☐ Satin
- ☐ Matte ☐ Semi gloss
- ☐ Eggshell ☐ High gloss

Notes

Date

Job Name _____ ph # _____

Job Address _____

Paint Brand _____

Room Name

Wall Color _____
- [ ] Flat
- [ ] Matte
- [ ] Eggshell
- [ ] Satin
- [ ] Semi gloss
- [ ] High gloss

Ceiling Color _____
- [ ] Flat
- [ ] Matte
- [ ] Eggshell
- [ ] Satin
- [ ] Semi gloss
- [ ] High gloss

Trim Color _____
- [ ] Flat
- [ ] Matte
- [ ] Eggshell
- [ ] Satin
- [ ] Semi gloss
- [ ] High gloss

Notes

Room Name

Wall Color _____
- [ ] Flat
- [ ] Matte
- [ ] Eggshell
- [ ] Satin
- [ ] Semi gloss
- [ ] High gloss

Ceiling Color _____
- [ ] Flat
- [ ] Matte
- [ ] Eggshell
- [ ] Satin
- [ ] Semi gloss
- [ ] High gloss

Trim Color _____
- [ ] Flat
- [ ] Matte
- [ ] Eggshell
- [ ] Satin
- [ ] Semi gloss
- [ ] High gloss

Notes

Date _____

Job Name _____ ph # _____

Job Address _____

Paint Brand _____

Room Name _____

Wall Color _____

- [ ] Flat   [ ] Satin
- [ ] Matte   [ ] Semi gloss
- [ ] Eggshell   [ ] High gloss

Ceiling Color _____

- [ ] Flat   [ ] Satin
- [ ] Matte   [ ] Semi gloss
- [ ] Eggshell   [ ] High gloss

Trim Color _____

- [ ] Flat   [ ] Satin
- [ ] Matte   [ ] Semi gloss
- [ ] Eggshell   [ ] High gloss

Notes

Room Name _____

Wall Color _____

- [ ] Flat   [ ] Satin
- [ ] Matte   [ ] Semi gloss
- [ ] Eggshell   [ ] High gloss

Ceiling Color _____

- [ ] Flat   [ ] Satin
- [ ] Matte   [ ] Semi gloss
- [ ] Eggshell   [ ] High gloss

Trim Color _____

- [ ] Flat   [ ] Satin
- [ ] Matte   [ ] Semi gloss
- [ ] Eggshell   [ ] High gloss

Notes

Date _____

Job Name _____ ph # _____

Job Address _____

Paint Brand _____

Room Name
_____

Wall Color _____
- ☐ Flat ☐ Satin
- ☐ Matte ☐ Semi gloss
- ☐ Eggshell ☐ High gloss

Ceiling Color _____
- ☐ Flat ☐ Satin
- ☐ Matte ☐ Semi gloss
- ☐ Eggshell ☐ High gloss

Trim Color _____
- ☐ Flat ☐ Satin
- ☐ Matte ☐ Semi gloss
- ☐ Eggshell ☐ High gloss

Notes

Room Name
_____

Wall Color _____
- ☐ Flat ☐ Satin
- ☐ Matte ☐ Semi gloss
- ☐ Eggshell ☐ High gloss

Ceiling Color _____
- ☐ Flat ☐ Satin
- ☐ Matte ☐ Semi gloss
- ☐ Eggshell ☐ High gloss

Trim Color _____
- ☐ Flat ☐ Satin
- ☐ Matte ☐ Semi gloss
- ☐ Eggshell ☐ High gloss

Notes

Date _____

Job Name _____ ph # _____

Job Address _____

Paint Brand _____

Room Name _____

☐ Flat	☐ Satin
☐ Matte	☐ Semi gloss
☐ Eggshell	☐ High gloss

Wall Color _____

☐ Flat	☐ Satin
☐ Matte	☐ Semi gloss
☐ Eggshell	☐ High gloss

Ceiling Color _____

☐ Flat	☐ Satin
☐ Matte	☐ Semi gloss
☐ Eggshell	☐ High gloss

Trim Color _____

Notes

Room Name _____

☐ Flat	☐ Satin
☐ Matte	☐ Semi gloss
☐ Eggshell	☐ High gloss

Wall Color _____

☐ Flat	☐ Satin
☐ Matte	☐ Semi gloss
☐ Eggshell	☐ High gloss

Ceiling Color _____

☐ Flat	☐ Satin
☐ Matte	☐ Semi gloss
☐ Eggshell	☐ High gloss

Trim Color _____

Notes

Date _____

Job Name _____ ph # _____

Job Address _____

Paint Brand _____

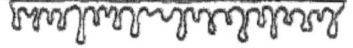

Room Name

Wall Color _____
- ☐ Flat ☐ Satin
- ☐ Matte ☐ Semi gloss
- ☐ Eggshell ☐ High gloss

Ceiling Color _____
- ☐ Flat ☐ Satin
- ☐ Matte ☐ Semi gloss
- ☐ Eggshell ☐ High gloss

Trim Color _____
- ☐ Flat ☐ Satin
- ☐ Matte ☐ Semi gloss
- ☐ Eggshell ☐ High gloss

Notes

Room Name

Wall Color _____
- ☐ Flat ☐ Satin
- ☐ Matte ☐ Semi gloss
- ☐ Eggshell ☐ High gloss

Ceiling Color _____
- ☐ Flat ☐ Satin
- ☐ Matte ☐ Semi gloss
- ☐ Eggshell ☐ High gloss

Trim Color _____
- ☐ Flat ☐ Satin
- ☐ Matte ☐ Semi gloss
- ☐ Eggshell ☐ High gloss

Notes

Date _____

Job Name _____ ph # _____

Job Address _____

Paint Brand _____

Room Name _____

Wall Color _____	☐ Flat ☐ Satin ☐ Matte ☐ Semi gloss ☐ Eggshell ☐ High gloss
Ceiling Color _____	☐ Flat ☐ Satin ☐ Matte ☐ Semi gloss ☐ Eggshell ☐ High gloss
Trim Color _____	☐ Flat ☐ Satin ☐ Matte ☐ Semi gloss ☐ Eggshell ☐ High gloss

Notes

Room Name _____

Wall Color _____	☐ Flat ☐ Satin ☐ Matte ☐ Semi gloss ☐ Eggshell ☐ High gloss
Ceiling Color _____	☐ Flat ☐ Satin ☐ Matte ☐ Semi gloss ☐ Eggshell ☐ High gloss
Trim Color _____	☐ Flat ☐ Satin ☐ Matte ☐ Semi gloss ☐ Eggshell ☐ High gloss

Notes

Date _____

Job Name _____   ph # _____

Job Address _____

Paint Brand _____

Room Name _____

Wall Color _____
- [ ] Flat
- [ ] Matte
- [ ] Eggshell
- [ ] Satin
- [ ] Semi gloss
- [ ] High gloss

Ceiling Color _____
- [ ] Flat
- [ ] Matte
- [ ] Eggshell
- [ ] Satin
- [ ] Semi gloss
- [ ] High gloss

Trim Color _____
- [ ] Flat
- [ ] Matte
- [ ] Eggshell
- [ ] Satin
- [ ] Semi gloss
- [ ] High gloss

Notes

Room Name _____

Wall Color _____
- [ ] Flat
- [ ] Matte
- [ ] Eggshell
- [ ] Satin
- [ ] Semi gloss
- [ ] High gloss

Ceiling Color _____
- [ ] Flat
- [ ] Matte
- [ ] Eggshell
- [ ] Satin
- [ ] Semi gloss
- [ ] High gloss

Trim Color _____
- [ ] Flat
- [ ] Matte
- [ ] Eggshell
- [ ] Satin
- [ ] Semi gloss
- [ ] High gloss

Notes

Date _____

Job Name _____ ph # _____

Job Address _____

Paint Brand _____

Room Name _____

☐ Flat	☐ Satin
☐ Matte	☐ Semi gloss
☐ Eggshell	☐ High gloss

Wall Color _____

☐ Flat	☐ Satin
☐ Matte	☐ Semi gloss
☐ Eggshell	☐ High gloss

Ceiling Color _____

☐ Flat	☐ Satin
☐ Matte	☐ Semi gloss
☐ Eggshell	☐ High gloss

Trim Color _____

Notes

Room Name _____

☐ Flat	☐ Satin
☐ Matte	☐ Semi gloss
☐ Eggshell	☐ High gloss

Wall Color _____

☐ Flat	☐ Satin
☐ Matte	☐ Semi gloss
☐ Eggshell	☐ High gloss

Ceiling Color _____

☐ Flat	☐ Satin
☐ Matte	☐ Semi gloss
☐ Eggshell	☐ High gloss

Trim Color _____

Notes

Date _____

Job Name _____ ph # _____

Job Address _____

Paint Brand _____

Room Name

Wall Color _____
☐ Flat ☐ Satin
☐ Matte ☐ Semi gloss
☐ Eggshell ☐ High gloss

Ceiling Color _____
☐ Flat ☐ Satin
☐ Matte ☐ Semi gloss
☐ Eggshell ☐ High gloss

Trim Color _____
☐ Flat ☐ Satin
☐ Matte ☐ Semi gloss
☐ Eggshell ☐ High gloss

Notes

Room Name

Wall Color _____
☐ Flat ☐ Satin
☐ Matte ☐ Semi gloss
☐ Eggshell ☐ High gloss

Ceiling Color _____
☐ Flat ☐ Satin
☐ Matte ☐ Semi gloss
☐ Eggshell ☐ High gloss

Trim Color _____
☐ Flat ☐ Satin
☐ Matte ☐ Semi gloss
☐ Eggshell ☐ High gloss

Notes

Date _____

Job Name _____ ph # _____

Job Address _____

Paint Brand _____

Room Name _____

Wall Color _____

- [ ] Flat
- [ ] Matte
- [ ] Eggshell
- [ ] Satin
- [ ] Semi gloss
- [ ] High gloss

Ceiling Color _____

- [ ] Flat
- [ ] Matte
- [ ] Eggshell
- [ ] Satin
- [ ] Semi gloss
- [ ] High gloss

Trim Color _____

- [ ] Flat
- [ ] Matte
- [ ] Eggshell
- [ ] Satin
- [ ] Semi gloss
- [ ] High gloss

Notes

Room Name _____

Wall Color _____

- [ ] Flat
- [ ] Matte
- [ ] Eggshell
- [ ] Satin
- [ ] Semi gloss
- [ ] High gloss

Ceiling Color _____

- [ ] Flat
- [ ] Matte
- [ ] Eggshell
- [ ] Satin
- [ ] Semi gloss
- [ ] High gloss

Trim Color _____

- [ ] Flat
- [ ] Matte
- [ ] Eggshell
- [ ] Satin
- [ ] Semi gloss
- [ ] High gloss

Notes

Date _____

Job Name _____ ph # _____

Job Address _____

Paint Brand _____

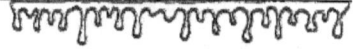

Room Name _____

Wall Color _____
- ☐ Flat ☐ Satin
- ☐ Matte ☐ Semi gloss
- ☐ Eggshell ☐ High gloss

Ceiling Color _____
- ☐ Flat ☐ Satin
- ☐ Matte ☐ Semi gloss
- ☐ Eggshell ☐ High gloss

Trim Color _____
- ☐ Flat ☐ Satin
- ☐ Matte ☐ Semi gloss
- ☐ Eggshell ☐ High gloss

Notes

Room Name _____

Wall Color _____
- ☐ Flat ☐ Satin
- ☐ Matte ☐ Semi gloss
- ☐ Eggshell ☐ High gloss

Ceiling Color _____
- ☐ Flat ☐ Satin
- ☐ Matte ☐ Semi gloss
- ☐ Eggshell ☐ High gloss

Trim Color _____
- ☐ Flat ☐ Satin
- ☐ Matte ☐ Semi gloss
- ☐ Eggshell ☐ High gloss

Notes

Date _____

Job Name _____ ph # _____

Job Address _____

Paint Brand _____

Room Name
_____

Wall Color _____

☐ Flat	☐ Satin
☐ Matte	☐ Semi gloss
☐ Eggshell	☐ High gloss

Ceiling Color _____

☐ Flat	☐ Satin
☐ Matte	☐ Semi gloss
☐ Eggshell	☐ High gloss

Trim Color _____

☐ Flat	☐ Satin
☐ Matte	☐ Semi gloss
☐ Eggshell	☐ High gloss

Notes

Room Name
_____

Wall Color _____

☐ Flat	☐ Satin
☐ Matte	☐ Semi gloss
☐ Eggshell	☐ High gloss

Ceiling Color _____

☐ Flat	☐ Satin
☐ Matte	☐ Semi gloss
☐ Eggshell	☐ High gloss

Trim Color _____

☐ Flat	☐ Satin
☐ Matte	☐ Semi gloss
☐ Eggshell	☐ High gloss

Notes

Date _____

Job Name _____ ph # _____

Job Address _____

Paint Brand _____

Room Name _____

Wall Color _____
- ☐ Flat ☐ Satin
- ☐ Matte ☐ Semi gloss
- ☐ Eggshell ☐ High gloss

Ceiling Color _____
- ☐ Flat ☐ Satin
- ☐ Matte ☐ Semi gloss
- ☐ Eggshell ☐ High gloss

Trim Color _____
- ☐ Flat ☐ Satin
- ☐ Matte ☐ Semi gloss
- ☐ Eggshell ☐ High gloss

Notes

Room Name _____

Wall Color _____
- ☐ Flat ☐ Satin
- ☐ Matte ☐ Semi gloss
- ☐ Eggshell ☐ High gloss

Ceiling Color _____
- ☐ Flat ☐ Satin
- ☐ Matte ☐ Semi gloss
- ☐ Eggshell ☐ High gloss

Trim Color _____
- ☐ Flat ☐ Satin
- ☐ Matte ☐ Semi gloss
- ☐ Eggshell ☐ High gloss

Notes

Date _____

Job Name _____   ph # _____

Job Address _____

Paint Brand _____

Room Name _____

Wall Color _____
- ☐ Flat   ☐ Satin
- ☐ Matte   ☐ Semi gloss
- ☐ Eggshell ☐ High gloss

Ceiling Color _____
- ☐ Flat   ☐ Satin
- ☐ Matte   ☐ Semi gloss
- ☐ Eggshell ☐ High gloss

Trim Color _____
- ☐ Flat   ☐ Satin
- ☐ Matte   ☐ Semi gloss
- ☐ Eggshell ☐ High gloss

Notes

Room Name _____

Wall Color _____
- ☐ Flat   ☐ Satin
- ☐ Matte   ☐ Semi gloss
- ☐ Eggshell ☐ High gloss

Ceiling Color _____
- ☐ Flat   ☐ Satin
- ☐ Matte   ☐ Semi gloss
- ☐ Eggshell ☐ High gloss

Trim Color _____
- ☐ Flat   ☐ Satin
- ☐ Matte   ☐ Semi gloss
- ☐ Eggshell ☐ High gloss

Notes

Date _____

Job Name _____   ph # _____

Job Address _____

Paint Brand _____

Room Name _____

Wall Color _____
- [ ] Flat
- [ ] Matte
- [ ] Eggshell
- [ ] Satin
- [ ] Semi gloss
- [ ] High gloss

Ceiling Color _____
- [ ] Flat
- [ ] Matte
- [ ] Eggshell
- [ ] Satin
- [ ] Semi gloss
- [ ] High gloss

Trim Color _____
- [ ] Flat
- [ ] Matte
- [ ] Eggshell
- [ ] Satin
- [ ] Semi gloss
- [ ] High gloss

Notes

Room Name _____

Wall Color _____
- [ ] Flat
- [ ] Matte
- [ ] Eggshell
- [ ] Satin
- [ ] Semi gloss
- [ ] High gloss

Ceiling Color _____
- [ ] Flat
- [ ] Matte
- [ ] Eggshell
- [ ] Satin
- [ ] Semi gloss
- [ ] High gloss

Trim Color _____
- [ ] Flat
- [ ] Matte
- [ ] Eggshell
- [ ] Satin
- [ ] Semi gloss
- [ ] High gloss

Notes

Date _____

Job Name _____ ph # _____

Job Address _____

Paint Brand _____

Room Name _____

Wall Color _____
- ☐ Flat ☐ Satin
- ☐ Matte ☐ Semi gloss
- ☐ Eggshell ☐ High gloss

Ceiling Color _____
- ☐ Flat ☐ Satin
- ☐ Matte ☐ Semi gloss
- ☐ Eggshell ☐ High gloss

Trim Color _____
- ☐ Flat ☐ Satin
- ☐ Matte ☐ Semi gloss
- ☐ Eggshell ☐ High gloss

Notes

Room Name _____

Wall Color _____
- ☐ Flat ☐ Satin
- ☐ Matte ☐ Semi gloss
- ☐ Eggshell ☐ High gloss

Ceiling Color _____
- ☐ Flat ☐ Satin
- ☐ Matte ☐ Semi gloss
- ☐ Eggshell ☐ High gloss

Trim Color _____
- ☐ Flat ☐ Satin
- ☐ Matte ☐ Semi gloss
- ☐ Eggshell ☐ High gloss

Notes

Date _____

Job Name _____   ph # _____

Job Address _____

Paint Brand _____

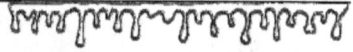

Room Name _____

	Flat ☐	Satin ☐
Wall Color	Matte ☐	Semi gloss ☐
	Eggshell ☐	High gloss ☐
	Flat ☐	Satin ☐
Ceiling Color	Matte ☐	Semi gloss ☐
	Eggshell ☐	High gloss ☐
	Flat ☐	Satin ☐
Trim Color	Matte ☐	Semi gloss ☐
	Eggshell ☐	High gloss ☐

Notes

Room Name _____

	Flat ☐	Satin ☐
Wall Color	Matte ☐	Semi gloss ☐
	Eggshell ☐	High gloss ☐
	Flat ☐	Satin ☐
Ceiling Color	Matte ☐	Semi gloss ☐
	Eggshell ☐	High gloss ☐
	Flat ☐	Satin ☐
Trim Color	Matte ☐	Semi gloss ☐
	Eggshell ☐	High gloss ☐

Notes

Date _____

Job Name _____   ph # _____

Job Address _____

Paint Brand _____

Room Name

Wall Color _____

☐ Flat   ☐ Satin
☐ Matte   ☐ Semi gloss
☐ Eggshell ☐ High gloss

Ceiling Color _____

☐ Flat   ☐ Satin
☐ Matte   ☐ Semi gloss
☐ Eggshell ☐ High gloss

Trim Color _____

☐ Flat   ☐ Satin
☐ Matte   ☐ Semi gloss
☐ Eggshell ☐ High gloss

Notes

Room Name

Wall Color _____

☐ Flat   ☐ Satin
☐ Matte   ☐ Semi gloss
☐ Eggshell ☐ High gloss

Ceiling Color _____

☐ Flat   ☐ Satin
☐ Matte   ☐ Semi gloss
☐ Eggshell ☐ High gloss

Trim Color _____

☐ Flat   ☐ Satin
☐ Matte   ☐ Semi gloss
☐ Eggshell ☐ High gloss

Notes

Date

Job Name _____ ph # _____

Job Address _____

Paint Brand _____

Room Name _____

Wall Color _____
- ☐ Flat ☐ Satin
- ☐ Matte ☐ Semi gloss
- ☐ Eggshell ☐ High gloss

Ceiling Color _____
- ☐ Flat ☐ Satin
- ☐ Matte ☐ Semi gloss
- ☐ Eggshell ☐ High gloss

Trim Color _____
- ☐ Flat ☐ Satin
- ☐ Matte ☐ Semi gloss
- ☐ Eggshell ☐ High gloss

Notes

Room Name _____

Wall Color _____
- ☐ Flat ☐ Satin
- ☐ Matte ☐ Semi gloss
- ☐ Eggshell ☐ High gloss

Ceiling Color _____
- ☐ Flat ☐ Satin
- ☐ Matte ☐ Semi gloss
- ☐ Eggshell ☐ High gloss

Trim Color _____
- ☐ Flat ☐ Satin
- ☐ Matte ☐ Semi gloss
- ☐ Eggshell ☐ High gloss

Notes

Date _____

Job Name _____ ph # _____

Job Address _____

Paint Brand _____

Room Name _____

Wall Color _____
- ☐ Flat   ☐ Satin
- ☐ Matte   ☐ Semi gloss
- ☐ Eggshell   ☐ High gloss

Ceiling Color _____
- ☐ Flat   ☐ Satin
- ☐ Matte   ☐ Semi gloss
- ☐ Eggshell   ☐ High gloss

Trim Color _____
- ☐ Flat   ☐ Satin
- ☐ Matte   ☐ Semi gloss
- ☐ Eggshell   ☐ High gloss

Notes

Room Name _____

Wall Color _____
- ☐ Flat   ☐ Satin
- ☐ Matte   ☐ Semi gloss
- ☐ Eggshell   ☐ High gloss

Ceiling Color _____
- ☐ Flat   ☐ Satin
- ☐ Matte   ☐ Semi gloss
- ☐ Eggshell   ☐ High gloss

Trim Color _____
- ☐ Flat   ☐ Satin
- ☐ Matte   ☐ Semi gloss
- ☐ Eggshell   ☐ High gloss

Notes

Date _____

Job Name _____ ph # _____

Job Address _____

Paint Brand _____

Room Name _____

Wall Color _____
- [ ] Flat   [ ] Satin
- [ ] Matte   [ ] Semi gloss
- [ ] Eggshell   [ ] High gloss

Ceiling Color _____
- [ ] Flat   [ ] Satin
- [ ] Matte   [ ] Semi gloss
- [ ] Eggshell   [ ] High gloss

Trim Color _____
- [ ] Flat   [ ] Satin
- [ ] Matte   [ ] Semi gloss
- [ ] Eggshell   [ ] High gloss

Notes
_____
_____
_____
_____
_____
_____

Room Name _____

Wall Color _____
- [ ] Flat   [ ] Satin
- [ ] Matte   [ ] Semi gloss
- [ ] Eggshell   [ ] High gloss

Ceiling Color _____
- [ ] Flat   [ ] Satin
- [ ] Matte   [ ] Semi gloss
- [ ] Eggshell   [ ] High gloss

Trim Color _____
- [ ] Flat   [ ] Satin
- [ ] Matte   [ ] Semi gloss
- [ ] Eggshell   [ ] High gloss

Notes
_____
_____
_____
_____
_____
_____

Date _____

Job Name _____ ph # _____

Job Address _____

Paint Brand _____

Room Name _____

Wall Color _____	☐ Flat ☐ Matte ☐ Eggshell	☐ Satin ☐ Semi gloss ☐ High gloss
Ceiling Color _____	☐ Flat ☐ Matte ☐ Eggshell	☐ Satin ☐ Semi gloss ☐ High gloss
Trim Color _____	☐ Flat ☐ Matte ☐ Eggshell	☐ Satin ☐ Semi gloss ☐ High gloss

Notes

Room Name _____

Wall Color _____	☐ Flat ☐ Matte ☐ Eggshell	☐ Satin ☐ Semi gloss ☐ High gloss
Ceiling Color _____	☐ Flat ☐ Matte ☐ Eggshell	☐ Satin ☐ Semi gloss ☐ High gloss
Trim Color _____	☐ Flat ☐ Matte ☐ Eggshell	☐ Satin ☐ Semi gloss ☐ High gloss

Notes

Date _____

Job Name _____ ph # _____

Job Address _____

Paint Brand _____

Room Name _____

Wall Color _____
- ☐ Flat ☐ Satin
- ☐ Matte ☐ Semi gloss
- ☐ Eggshell ☐ High gloss

Ceiling Color _____
- ☐ Flat ☐ Satin
- ☐ Matte ☐ Semi gloss
- ☐ Eggshell ☐ High gloss

Trim Color _____
- ☐ Flat ☐ Satin
- ☐ Matte ☐ Semi gloss
- ☐ Eggshell ☐ High gloss

Notes

Room Name _____

Wall Color _____
- ☐ Flat ☐ Satin
- ☐ Matte ☐ Semi gloss
- ☐ Eggshell ☐ High gloss

Ceiling Color _____
- ☐ Flat ☐ Satin
- ☐ Matte ☐ Semi gloss
- ☐ Eggshell ☐ High gloss

Trim Color _____
- ☐ Flat ☐ Satin
- ☐ Matte ☐ Semi gloss
- ☐ Eggshell ☐ High gloss

Notes

Date _____

Job Name _____ ph # _____

Job Address _____

Paint Brand _____

Room Name
_____

Wall Color _____
- ☐ Flat   ☐ Satin
- ☐ Matte   ☐ Semi gloss
- ☐ Eggshell   ☐ High gloss

Ceiling Color _____
- ☐ Flat   ☐ Satin
- ☐ Matte   ☐ Semi gloss
- ☐ Eggshell   ☐ High gloss

Trim Color _____
- ☐ Flat   ☐ Satin
- ☐ Matte   ☐ Semi gloss
- ☐ Eggshell   ☐ High gloss

Notes

Room Name
_____

Wall Color _____
- ☐ Flat   ☐ Satin
- ☐ Matte   ☐ Semi gloss
- ☐ Eggshell   ☐ High gloss

Ceiling Color _____
- ☐ Flat   ☐ Satin
- ☐ Matte   ☐ Semi gloss
- ☐ Eggshell   ☐ High gloss

Trim Color _____
- ☐ Flat   ☐ Satin
- ☐ Matte   ☐ Semi gloss
- ☐ Eggshell   ☐ High gloss

Notes

Date _____

Job Name _____ ph # _____

Job Address _____

Paint Brand _____

Room Name

Wall Color _____

- ☐ Flat   ☐ Satin
- ☐ Matte   ☐ Semi gloss
- ☐ Eggshell ☐ High gloss

Ceiling Color _____

- ☐ Flat   ☐ Satin
- ☐ Matte   ☐ Semi gloss
- ☐ Eggshell ☐ High gloss

Trim Color _____

- ☐ Flat   ☐ Satin
- ☐ Matte   ☐ Semi gloss
- ☐ Eggshell ☐ High gloss

Notes

Room Name

Wall Color _____

- ☐ Flat   ☐ Satin
- ☐ Matte   ☐ Semi gloss
- ☐ Eggshell ☐ High gloss

Ceiling Color _____

- ☐ Flat   ☐ Satin
- ☐ Matte   ☐ Semi gloss
- ☐ Eggshell ☐ High gloss

Trim Color _____

- ☐ Flat   ☐ Satin
- ☐ Matte   ☐ Semi gloss
- ☐ Eggshell ☐ High gloss

Notes

Date _____

Job Name _____   ph # _____

Job Address _____

Paint Brand _____

Room Name

Wall Color _____
- [ ] Flat
- [ ] Matte
- [ ] Eggshell
- [ ] Satin
- [ ] Semi gloss
- [ ] High gloss

Ceiling Color _____
- [ ] Flat
- [ ] Matte
- [ ] Eggshell
- [ ] Satin
- [ ] Semi gloss
- [ ] High gloss

Trim Color _____
- [ ] Flat
- [ ] Matte
- [ ] Eggshell
- [ ] Satin
- [ ] Semi gloss
- [ ] High gloss

Notes

Room Name

Wall Color _____
- [ ] Flat
- [ ] Matte
- [ ] Eggshell
- [ ] Satin
- [ ] Semi gloss
- [ ] High gloss

Ceiling Color _____
- [ ] Flat
- [ ] Matte
- [ ] Eggshell
- [ ] Satin
- [ ] Semi gloss
- [ ] High gloss

Trim Color _____
- [ ] Flat
- [ ] Matte
- [ ] Eggshell
- [ ] Satin
- [ ] Semi gloss
- [ ] High gloss

Notes

Date _____

Job Name _____ ph # _____

Job Address _____

Paint Brand _____

Room Name _____

Wall Color _____
- ☐ Flat ☐ Satin
- ☐ Matte ☐ Semi gloss
- ☐ Eggshell ☐ High gloss

Ceiling Color _____
- ☐ Flat ☐ Satin
- ☐ Matte ☐ Semi gloss
- ☐ Eggshell ☐ High gloss

Trim Color _____
- ☐ Flat ☐ Satin
- ☐ Matte ☐ Semi gloss
- ☐ Eggshell ☐ High gloss

Notes

Room Name _____

Wall Color _____
- ☐ Flat ☐ Satin
- ☐ Matte ☐ Semi gloss
- ☐ Eggshell ☐ High gloss

Ceiling Color _____
- ☐ Flat ☐ Satin
- ☐ Matte ☐ Semi gloss
- ☐ Eggshell ☐ High gloss

Trim Color _____
- ☐ Flat ☐ Satin
- ☐ Matte ☐ Semi gloss
- ☐ Eggshell ☐ High gloss

Notes

Date _____

Job Name _____ ph # _____

Job Address _____

Paint Brand _____

Room Name _____

Wall Color _____

☐ Flat	☐ Satin
☐ Matte	☐ Semi gloss
☐ Eggshell	☐ High gloss

Ceiling Color _____

☐ Flat	☐ Satin
☐ Matte	☐ Semi gloss
☐ Eggshell	☐ High gloss

Trim Color _____

☐ Flat	☐ Satin
☐ Matte	☐ Semi gloss
☐ Eggshell	☐ High gloss

Notes

Room Name _____

Wall Color _____

☐ Flat	☐ Satin
☐ Matte	☐ Semi gloss
☐ Eggshell	☐ High gloss

Ceiling Color _____

☐ Flat	☐ Satin
☐ Matte	☐ Semi gloss
☐ Eggshell	☐ High gloss

Trim Color _____

☐ Flat	☐ Satin
☐ Matte	☐ Semi gloss
☐ Eggshell	☐ High gloss

Notes

Date _____

Job Name _____ ph # _____

Job Address _____

Paint Brand _____

Room Name _____

Wall Color _____
- ☐ Flat ☐ Satin
- ☐ Matte ☐ Semi gloss
- ☐ Eggshell ☐ High gloss

Ceiling Color _____
- ☐ Flat ☐ Satin
- ☐ Matte ☐ Semi gloss
- ☐ Eggshell ☐ High gloss

Trim Color _____
- ☐ Flat ☐ Satin
- ☐ Matte ☐ Semi gloss
- ☐ Eggshell ☐ High gloss

Notes

Room Name _____

Wall Color _____
- ☐ Flat ☐ Satin
- ☐ Matte ☐ Semi gloss
- ☐ Eggshell ☐ High gloss

Ceiling Color _____
- ☐ Flat ☐ Satin
- ☐ Matte ☐ Semi gloss
- ☐ Eggshell ☐ High gloss

Trim Color _____
- ☐ Flat ☐ Satin
- ☐ Matte ☐ Semi gloss
- ☐ Eggshell ☐ High gloss

Notes

Date _____

Job Name _____ ph # _____

Job Address _____

Paint Brand _____

Room Name _____

Wall Color _____

☐ Flat	☐ Satin
☐ Matte	☐ Semi gloss
☐ Eggshell	☐ High gloss

Ceiling Color _____

☐ Flat	☐ Satin
☐ Matte	☐ Semi gloss
☐ Eggshell	☐ High gloss

Trim Color _____

☐ Flat	☐ Satin
☐ Matte	☐ Semi gloss
☐ Eggshell	☐ High gloss

Notes

Room Name _____

Wall Color _____

☐ Flat	☐ Satin
☐ Matte	☐ Semi gloss
☐ Eggshell	☐ High gloss

Ceiling Color _____

☐ Flat	☐ Satin
☐ Matte	☐ Semi gloss
☐ Eggshell	☐ High gloss

Trim Color _____

☐ Flat	☐ Satin
☐ Matte	☐ Semi gloss
☐ Eggshell	☐ High gloss

Notes

Date _____

Job Name _____ ph # _____

Job Address _____

Paint Brand _____

Room Name

Wall Color _____
- ☐ Flat ☐ Satin
- ☐ Matte ☐ Semi gloss
- ☐ Eggshell ☐ High gloss

Ceiling Color _____
- ☐ Flat ☐ Satin
- ☐ Matte ☐ Semi gloss
- ☐ Eggshell ☐ High gloss

Trim Color _____
- ☐ Flat ☐ Satin
- ☐ Matte ☐ Semi gloss
- ☐ Eggshell ☐ High gloss

Notes

Room Name

Wall Color _____
- ☐ Flat ☐ Satin
- ☐ Matte ☐ Semi gloss
- ☐ Eggshell ☐ High gloss

Ceiling Color _____
- ☐ Flat ☐ Satin
- ☐ Matte ☐ Semi gloss
- ☐ Eggshell ☐ High gloss

Trim Color _____
- ☐ Flat ☐ Satin
- ☐ Matte ☐ Semi gloss
- ☐ Eggshell ☐ High gloss

Notes

Date _____

Job Name _____ ph # _____

Job Address _____

Paint Brand _____

Room Name _____

Wall Color _____

☐ Flat ☐ Satin
☐ Matte ☐ Semi gloss
☐ Eggshell ☐ High gloss

Ceiling Color _____

☐ Flat ☐ Satin
☐ Matte ☐ Semi gloss
☐ Eggshell ☐ High gloss

Trim Color _____

☐ Flat ☐ Satin
☐ Matte ☐ Semi gloss
☐ Eggshell ☐ High gloss

Notes

Room Name _____

Wall Color _____

☐ Flat ☐ Satin
☐ Matte ☐ Semi gloss
☐ Eggshell ☐ High gloss

Ceiling Color _____

☐ Flat ☐ Satin
☐ Matte ☐ Semi gloss
☐ Eggshell ☐ High gloss

Trim Color _____

☐ Flat ☐ Satin
☐ Matte ☐ Semi gloss
☐ Eggshell ☐ High gloss

Notes

Date _____

Job Name _____ ph # _____

Job Address _____

Paint Brand _____

Room Name _____

Wall Color _____
☐ Flat ☐ Satin
☐ Matte ☐ Semi gloss
☐ Eggshell ☐ High gloss

Ceiling Color _____
☐ Flat ☐ Satin
☐ Matte ☐ Semi gloss
☐ Eggshell ☐ High gloss

Trim Color _____
☐ Flat ☐ Satin
☐ Matte ☐ Semi gloss
☐ Eggshell ☐ High gloss

Notes

Room Name _____

Wall Color _____
☐ Flat ☐ Satin
☐ Matte ☐ Semi gloss
☐ Eggshell ☐ High gloss

Ceiling Color _____
☐ Flat ☐ Satin
☐ Matte ☐ Semi gloss
☐ Eggshell ☐ High gloss

Trim Color _____
☐ Flat ☐ Satin
☐ Matte ☐ Semi gloss
☐ Eggshell ☐ High gloss

Notes

Date _____

Job Name _____ ph # _____

Job Address _____

Paint Brand _____

Room Name _____

Wall Color _____
- ☐ Flat
- ☐ Matte
- ☐ Eggshell
- ☐ Satin
- ☐ Semi gloss
- ☐ High gloss

Ceiling Color _____
- ☐ Flat
- ☐ Matte
- ☐ Eggshell
- ☐ Satin
- ☐ Semi gloss
- ☐ High gloss

Trim Color _____
- ☐ Flat
- ☐ Matte
- ☐ Eggshell
- ☐ Satin
- ☐ Semi gloss
- ☐ High gloss

Notes

Room Name _____

Wall Color _____
- ☐ Flat
- ☐ Matte
- ☐ Eggshell
- ☐ Satin
- ☐ Semi gloss
- ☐ High gloss

Ceiling Color _____
- ☐ Flat
- ☐ Matte
- ☐ Eggshell
- ☐ Satin
- ☐ Semi gloss
- ☐ High gloss

Trim Color _____
- ☐ Flat
- ☐ Matte
- ☐ Eggshell
- ☐ Satin
- ☐ Semi gloss
- ☐ High gloss

Notes

Date _____

Job Name _____ ph # _____

Job Address _____

Paint Brand _____
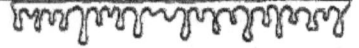

Room Name

Wall Color	☐ Flat	☐ Satin
	☐ Matte	☐ Semi gloss
	☐ Eggshell	☐ High gloss

Ceiling Color	☐ Flat	☐ Satin
	☐ Matte	☐ Semi gloss
	☐ Eggshell	☐ High gloss

Trim Color	☐ Flat	☐ Satin
	☐ Matte	☐ Semi gloss
	☐ Eggshell	☐ High gloss

Notes

Room Name

Wall Color	☐ Flat	☐ Satin
	☐ Matte	☐ Semi gloss
	☐ Eggshell	☐ High gloss

Ceiling Color	☐ Flat	☐ Satin
	☐ Matte	☐ Semi gloss
	☐ Eggshell	☐ High gloss

Trim Color	☐ Flat	☐ Satin
	☐ Matte	☐ Semi gloss
	☐ Eggshell	☐ High gloss

Notes

Date _____

Job Name _____ ph # _____

Job Address _____

Paint Brand _____

Room Name _____

Wall Color _____

- ☐ Flat ☐ Satin
- ☐ Matte ☐ Semi gloss
- ☐ Eggshell ☐ High gloss

Ceiling Color _____

- ☐ Flat ☐ Satin
- ☐ Matte ☐ Semi gloss
- ☐ Eggshell ☐ High gloss

Trim Color _____

- ☐ Flat ☐ Satin
- ☐ Matte ☐ Semi gloss
- ☐ Eggshell ☐ High gloss

Notes

Room Name _____

Wall Color _____

- ☐ Flat ☐ Satin
- ☐ Matte ☐ Semi gloss
- ☐ Eggshell ☐ High gloss

Ceiling Color _____

- ☐ Flat ☐ Satin
- ☐ Matte ☐ Semi gloss
- ☐ Eggshell ☐ High gloss

Trim Color _____

- ☐ Flat ☐ Satin
- ☐ Matte ☐ Semi gloss
- ☐ Eggshell ☐ High gloss

Notes

Date _____

Job Name _____ ph # _____

Job Address _____

Paint Brand _____

Room Name _____

Wall Color _____
- ☐ Flat ☐ Satin
- ☐ Matte ☐ Semi gloss
- ☐ Eggshell ☐ High gloss

Ceiling Color _____
- ☐ Flat ☐ Satin
- ☐ Matte ☐ Semi gloss
- ☐ Eggshell ☐ High gloss

Trim Color _____
- ☐ Flat ☐ Satin
- ☐ Matte ☐ Semi gloss
- ☐ Eggshell ☐ High gloss

Notes

Room Name _____

Wall Color _____
- ☐ Flat ☐ Satin
- ☐ Matte ☐ Semi gloss
- ☐ Eggshell ☐ High gloss

Ceiling Color _____
- ☐ Flat ☐ Satin
- ☐ Matte ☐ Semi gloss
- ☐ Eggshell ☐ High gloss

Trim Color _____
- ☐ Flat ☐ Satin
- ☐ Matte ☐ Semi gloss
- ☐ Eggshell ☐ High gloss

Notes

Date _____

Job Name _____ ph # _____

Job Address _____

Paint Brand _____

Room Name
_____

Wall Color _____
- ☐ Flat   ☐ Satin
- ☐ Matte   ☐ Semi gloss
- ☐ Eggshell   ☐ High gloss

Ceiling Color _____
- ☐ Flat   ☐ Satin
- ☐ Matte   ☐ Semi gloss
- ☐ Eggshell   ☐ High gloss

Trim Color _____
- ☐ Flat   ☐ Satin
- ☐ Matte   ☐ Semi gloss
- ☐ Eggshell   ☐ High gloss

Notes

Room Name
_____

Wall Color _____
- ☐ Flat   ☐ Satin
- ☐ Matte   ☐ Semi gloss
- ☐ Eggshell   ☐ High gloss

Ceiling Color _____
- ☐ Flat   ☐ Satin
- ☐ Matte   ☐ Semi gloss
- ☐ Eggshell   ☐ High gloss

Trim Color _____
- ☐ Flat   ☐ Satin
- ☐ Matte   ☐ Semi gloss
- ☐ Eggshell   ☐ High gloss

Notes

Date _____

Job Name _____ ph # _____

Job Address _____

Paint Brand _____

Room Name _____

Wall Color _____
- [ ] Flat
- [ ] Matte
- [ ] Eggshell
- [ ] Satin
- [ ] Semi gloss
- [ ] High gloss

Ceiling Color _____
- [ ] Flat
- [ ] Matte
- [ ] Eggshell
- [ ] Satin
- [ ] Semi gloss
- [ ] High gloss

Trim Color _____
- [ ] Flat
- [ ] Matte
- [ ] Eggshell
- [ ] Satin
- [ ] Semi gloss
- [ ] High gloss

Notes

Room Name _____

Wall Color _____
- [ ] Flat
- [ ] Matte
- [ ] Eggshell
- [ ] Satin
- [ ] Semi gloss
- [ ] High gloss

Ceiling Color _____
- [ ] Flat
- [ ] Matte
- [ ] Eggshell
- [ ] Satin
- [ ] Semi gloss
- [ ] High gloss

Trim Color _____
- [ ] Flat
- [ ] Matte
- [ ] Eggshell
- [ ] Satin
- [ ] Semi gloss
- [ ] High gloss

Notes

Date _____

Job Name _____ ph # _____

Job Address _____

Paint Brand _____

Room Name _____

Wall Color	☐ Flat ☐ Matte ☐ Eggshell	☐ Satin ☐ Semi gloss ☐ High gloss
Ceiling Color	☐ Flat ☐ Matte ☐ Eggshell	☐ Satin ☐ Semi gloss ☐ High gloss
Trim Color	☐ Flat ☐ Matte ☐ Eggshell	☐ Satin ☐ Semi gloss ☐ High gloss

Notes

Room Name _____

Wall Color	☐ Flat ☐ Matte ☐ Eggshell	☐ Satin ☐ Semi gloss ☐ High gloss
Ceiling Color	☐ Flat ☐ Matte ☐ Eggshell	☐ Satin ☐ Semi gloss ☐ High gloss
Trim Color	☐ Flat ☐ Matte ☐ Eggshell	☐ Satin ☐ Semi gloss ☐ High gloss

Notes

Date _____

Job Name _____ ph # _____

Job Address _____

Paint Brand _____

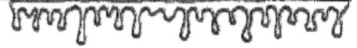

Room Name _____

Wall Color _____
- ☐ Flat ☐ Satin
- ☐ Matte ☐ Semi gloss
- ☐ Eggshell ☐ High gloss

Ceiling Color _____
- ☐ Flat ☐ Satin
- ☐ Matte ☐ Semi gloss
- ☐ Eggshell ☐ High gloss

Trim Color _____
- ☐ Flat ☐ Satin
- ☐ Matte ☐ Semi gloss
- ☐ Eggshell ☐ High gloss

Notes

Room Name _____

Wall Color _____
- ☐ Flat ☐ Satin
- ☐ Matte ☐ Semi gloss
- ☐ Eggshell ☐ High gloss

Ceiling Color _____
- ☐ Flat ☐ Satin
- ☐ Matte ☐ Semi gloss
- ☐ Eggshell ☐ High gloss

Trim Color _____
- ☐ Flat ☐ Satin
- ☐ Matte ☐ Semi gloss
- ☐ Eggshell ☐ High gloss

Notes

Date _____

Job Name _____ ph # _____

Job Address _____

Paint Brand _____

Room Name _____

Wall Color _____
- ☐ Flat   ☐ Satin
- ☐ Matte   ☐ Semi gloss
- ☐ Eggshell   ☐ High gloss

Ceiling Color _____
- ☐ Flat   ☐ Satin
- ☐ Matte   ☐ Semi gloss
- ☐ Eggshell   ☐ High gloss

Trim Color _____
- ☐ Flat   ☐ Satin
- ☐ Matte   ☐ Semi gloss
- ☐ Eggshell   ☐ High gloss

Notes

Room Name _____

Wall Color _____
- ☐ Flat   ☐ Satin
- ☐ Matte   ☐ Semi gloss
- ☐ Eggshell   ☐ High gloss

Ceiling Color _____
- ☐ Flat   ☐ Satin
- ☐ Matte   ☐ Semi gloss
- ☐ Eggshell   ☐ High gloss

Trim Color _____
- ☐ Flat   ☐ Satin
- ☐ Matte   ☐ Semi gloss
- ☐ Eggshell   ☐ High gloss

Notes

Date _____

Job Name _____ ph # _____

Job Address _____

Paint Brand _____

Room Name _____

Wall Color _____
☐ Flat ☐ Satin
☐ Matte ☐ Semi gloss
☐ Eggshell ☐ High gloss

Ceiling Color _____
☐ Flat ☐ Satin
☐ Matte ☐ Semi gloss
☐ Eggshell ☐ High gloss

Trim Color _____
☐ Flat ☐ Satin
☐ Matte ☐ Semi gloss
☐ Eggshell ☐ High gloss

Notes

Room Name _____

Wall Color _____
☐ Flat ☐ Satin
☐ Matte ☐ Semi gloss
☐ Eggshell ☐ High gloss

Ceiling Color _____
☐ Flat ☐ Satin
☐ Matte ☐ Semi gloss
☐ Eggshell ☐ High gloss

Trim Color _____
☐ Flat ☐ Satin
☐ Matte ☐ Semi gloss
☐ Eggshell ☐ High gloss

Notes

Date _____

Job Name _____ ph # _____

Job Address _____

Paint Brand _____

Room Name

Wall Color _____

☐ Flat	☐ Satin
☐ Matte	☐ Semi gloss
☐ Eggshell	☐ High gloss

Ceiling Color _____

☐ Flat	☐ Satin
☐ Matte	☐ Semi gloss
☐ Eggshell	☐ High gloss

Trim Color _____

☐ Flat	☐ Satin
☐ Matte	☐ Semi gloss
☐ Eggshell	☐ High gloss

Notes

Room Name

Wall Color _____

☐ Flat	☐ Satin
☐ Matte	☐ Semi gloss
☐ Eggshell	☐ High gloss

Ceiling Color _____

☐ Flat	☐ Satin
☐ Matte	☐ Semi gloss
☐ Eggshell	☐ High gloss

Trim Color _____

☐ Flat	☐ Satin
☐ Matte	☐ Semi gloss
☐ Eggshell	☐ High gloss

Notes

Date _____

Job Name _____ ph # _____

Job Address _____

Paint Brand _____

Room Name _____

Wall Color _____
- ☐ Flat ☐ Satin
- ☐ Matte ☐ Semi gloss
- ☐ Eggshell ☐ High gloss

Ceiling Color _____
- ☐ Flat ☐ Satin
- ☐ Matte ☐ Semi gloss
- ☐ Eggshell ☐ High gloss

Trim Color _____
- ☐ Flat ☐ Satin
- ☐ Matte ☐ Semi gloss
- ☐ Eggshell ☐ High gloss

Notes

Room Name _____

Wall Color _____
- ☐ Flat ☐ Satin
- ☐ Matte ☐ Semi gloss
- ☐ Eggshell ☐ High gloss

Ceiling Color _____
- ☐ Flat ☐ Satin
- ☐ Matte ☐ Semi gloss
- ☐ Eggshell ☐ High gloss

Trim Color _____
- ☐ Flat ☐ Satin
- ☐ Matte ☐ Semi gloss
- ☐ Eggshell ☐ High gloss

Notes

Date _____

Job Name _____ ph # _____

Job Address _____

Paint Brand _____

Room Name _____

Wall Color _____

- ☐ Flat ☐ Satin
- ☐ Matte ☐ Semi gloss
- ☐ Eggshell ☐ High gloss

Ceiling Color _____

- ☐ Flat ☐ Satin
- ☐ Matte ☐ Semi gloss
- ☐ Eggshell ☐ High gloss

Trim Color _____

- ☐ Flat ☐ Satin
- ☐ Matte ☐ Semi gloss
- ☐ Eggshell ☐ High gloss

Notes

Room Name _____

Wall Color _____

- ☐ Flat ☐ Satin
- ☐ Matte ☐ Semi gloss
- ☐ Eggshell ☐ High gloss

Ceiling Color _____

- ☐ Flat ☐ Satin
- ☐ Matte ☐ Semi gloss
- ☐ Eggshell ☐ High gloss

Trim Color _____

- ☐ Flat ☐ Satin
- ☐ Matte ☐ Semi gloss
- ☐ Eggshell ☐ High gloss

Notes

Date _____

Job Name _____ ph # _____

Job Address _____

Paint Brand _____

Room Name _____

Wall Color _____
- [ ] Flat
- [ ] Matte
- [ ] Eggshell
- [ ] Satin
- [ ] Semi gloss
- [ ] High gloss

Ceiling Color _____
- [ ] Flat
- [ ] Matte
- [ ] Eggshell
- [ ] Satin
- [ ] Semi gloss
- [ ] High gloss

Trim Color _____
- [ ] Flat
- [ ] Matte
- [ ] Eggshell
- [ ] Satin
- [ ] Semi gloss
- [ ] High gloss

Notes

Room Name _____

Wall Color _____
- [ ] Flat
- [ ] Matte
- [ ] Eggshell
- [ ] Satin
- [ ] Semi gloss
- [ ] High gloss

Ceiling Color _____
- [ ] Flat
- [ ] Matte
- [ ] Eggshell
- [ ] Satin
- [ ] Semi gloss
- [ ] High gloss

Trim Color _____
- [ ] Flat
- [ ] Matte
- [ ] Eggshell
- [ ] Satin
- [ ] Semi gloss
- [ ] High gloss

Notes

Date _____

Job Name _____ ph # _____

Job Address _____

Paint Brand _____

Room Name _____

Wall Color _____
☐ Flat ☐ Satin
☐ Matte ☐ Semi gloss
☐ Eggshell ☐ High gloss

Ceiling Color _____
☐ Flat ☐ Satin
☐ Matte ☐ Semi gloss
☐ Eggshell ☐ High gloss

Trim Color _____
☐ Flat ☐ Satin
☐ Matte ☐ Semi gloss
☐ Eggshell ☐ High gloss

Notes

Room Name _____

Wall Color _____
☐ Flat ☐ Satin
☐ Matte ☐ Semi gloss
☐ Eggshell ☐ High gloss

Ceiling Color _____
☐ Flat ☐ Satin
☐ Matte ☐ Semi gloss
☐ Eggshell ☐ High gloss

Trim Color _____
☐ Flat ☐ Satin
☐ Matte ☐ Semi gloss
☐ Eggshell ☐ High gloss

Notes

Date _____

Job Name _____   ph # _____

Job Address _____

Paint Brand _____

Room Name _____

Wall Color _____
- [ ] Flat
- [ ] Matte
- [ ] Eggshell
- [ ] Satin
- [ ] Semi gloss
- [ ] High gloss

Ceiling Color _____
- [ ] Flat
- [ ] Matte
- [ ] Eggshell
- [ ] Satin
- [ ] Semi gloss
- [ ] High gloss

Trim Color _____
- [ ] Flat
- [ ] Matte
- [ ] Eggshell
- [ ] Satin
- [ ] Semi gloss
- [ ] High gloss

Notes

Room Name _____

Wall Color _____
- [ ] Flat
- [ ] Matte
- [ ] Eggshell
- [ ] Satin
- [ ] Semi gloss
- [ ] High gloss

Ceiling Color _____
- [ ] Flat
- [ ] Matte
- [ ] Eggshell
- [ ] Satin
- [ ] Semi gloss
- [ ] High gloss

Trim Color _____
- [ ] Flat
- [ ] Matte
- [ ] Eggshell
- [ ] Satin
- [ ] Semi gloss
- [ ] High gloss

Notes

Date _____

Job Name _____ ph # _____

Job Address _____

Paint Brand _____

Room Name
_____

Wall Color _____
☐ Flat   ☐ Satin
☐ Matte   ☐ Semi gloss
☐ Eggshell ☐ High gloss

Ceiling Color _____
☐ Flat   ☐ Satin
☐ Matte   ☐ Semi gloss
☐ Eggshell ☐ High gloss

Trim Color _____
☐ Flat   ☐ Satin
☐ Matte   ☐ Semi gloss
☐ Eggshell ☐ High gloss

Notes

Room Name
_____

Wall Color _____
☐ Flat   ☐ Satin
☐ Matte   ☐ Semi gloss
☐ Eggshell ☐ High gloss

Ceiling Color _____
☐ Flat   ☐ Satin
☐ Matte   ☐ Semi gloss
☐ Eggshell ☐ High gloss

Trim Color _____
☐ Flat   ☐ Satin
☐ Matte   ☐ Semi gloss
☐ Eggshell ☐ High gloss

Notes

Date _____

Job Name _____ ph # _____

Job Address _____

Paint Brand _____

Room Name

Wall Color _____
- ☐ Flat ☐ Satin
- ☐ Matte ☐ Semi gloss
- ☐ Eggshell ☐ High gloss

Ceiling Color _____
- ☐ Flat ☐ Satin
- ☐ Matte ☐ Semi gloss
- ☐ Eggshell ☐ High gloss

Trim Color _____
- ☐ Flat ☐ Satin
- ☐ Matte ☐ Semi gloss
- ☐ Eggshell ☐ High gloss

Notes

Room Name

Wall Color _____
- ☐ Flat ☐ Satin
- ☐ Matte ☐ Semi gloss
- ☐ Eggshell ☐ High gloss

Ceiling Color _____
- ☐ Flat ☐ Satin
- ☐ Matte ☐ Semi gloss
- ☐ Eggshell ☐ High gloss

Trim Color _____
- ☐ Flat ☐ Satin
- ☐ Matte ☐ Semi gloss
- ☐ Eggshell ☐ High gloss

Notes

Date _____

Job Name _____ ph # _____

Job Address _____

Paint Brand _____

Room Name _____

Wall Color _____

☐ Flat   ☐ Satin
☐ Matte   ☐ Semi gloss
☐ Eggshell ☐ High gloss

Ceiling Color _____

☐ Flat   ☐ Satin
☐ Matte   ☐ Semi gloss
☐ Eggshell ☐ High gloss

Trim Color _____

☐ Flat   ☐ Satin
☐ Matte   ☐ Semi gloss
☐ Eggshell ☐ High gloss

Notes

Room Name _____

Wall Color _____

☐ Flat   ☐ Satin
☐ Matte   ☐ Semi gloss
☐ Eggshell ☐ High gloss

Ceiling Color _____

☐ Flat   ☐ Satin
☐ Matte   ☐ Semi gloss
☐ Eggshell ☐ High gloss

Trim Color _____

☐ Flat   ☐ Satin
☐ Matte   ☐ Semi gloss
☐ Eggshell ☐ High gloss

Notes

Date _____

Job Name _____ ph # _____

Job Address _____

Paint Brand _____

Room Name _____

Wall Color _____
- ☐ Flat ☐ Satin
- ☐ Matte ☐ Semi gloss
- ☐ Eggshell ☐ High gloss

Ceiling Color _____
- ☐ Flat ☐ Satin
- ☐ Matte ☐ Semi gloss
- ☐ Eggshell ☐ High gloss

Trim Color _____
- ☐ Flat ☐ Satin
- ☐ Matte ☐ Semi gloss
- ☐ Eggshell ☐ High gloss

Notes

Room Name _____

Wall Color _____
- ☐ Flat ☐ Satin
- ☐ Matte ☐ Semi gloss
- ☐ Eggshell ☐ High gloss

Ceiling Color _____
- ☐ Flat ☐ Satin
- ☐ Matte ☐ Semi gloss
- ☐ Eggshell ☐ High gloss

Trim Color _____
- ☐ Flat ☐ Satin
- ☐ Matte ☐ Semi gloss
- ☐ Eggshell ☐ High gloss

Notes

Date _____

Job Name _____ ph # _____

Job Address _____

Paint Brand _____

Room Name _____

Wall Color _____
- ☐ Flat ☐ Satin
- ☐ Matte ☐ Semi gloss
- ☐ Eggshell ☐ High gloss

Ceiling Color _____
- ☐ Flat ☐ Satin
- ☐ Matte ☐ Semi gloss
- ☐ Eggshell ☐ High gloss

Trim Color _____
- ☐ Flat ☐ Satin
- ☐ Matte ☐ Semi gloss
- ☐ Eggshell ☐ High gloss

Notes

Room Name _____

Wall Color _____
- ☐ Flat ☐ Satin
- ☐ Matte ☐ Semi gloss
- ☐ Eggshell ☐ High gloss

Ceiling Color _____
- ☐ Flat ☐ Satin
- ☐ Matte ☐ Semi gloss
- ☐ Eggshell ☐ High gloss

Trim Color _____
- ☐ Flat ☐ Satin
- ☐ Matte ☐ Semi gloss
- ☐ Eggshell ☐ High gloss

Notes

Date _____

Job Name _____ ph # _____

Job Address _____

Paint Brand _____

Room Name _____

Wall Color _____
- [ ] Flat
- [ ] Matte
- [ ] Eggshell
- [ ] Satin
- [ ] Semi gloss
- [ ] High gloss

Ceiling Color _____
- [ ] Flat
- [ ] Matte
- [ ] Eggshell
- [ ] Satin
- [ ] Semi gloss
- [ ] High gloss

Trim Color _____
- [ ] Flat
- [ ] Matte
- [ ] Eggshell
- [ ] Satin
- [ ] Semi gloss
- [ ] High gloss

Notes

Room Name _____

Wall Color _____
- [ ] Flat
- [ ] Matte
- [ ] Eggshell
- [ ] Satin
- [ ] Semi gloss
- [ ] High gloss

Ceiling Color _____
- [ ] Flat
- [ ] Matte
- [ ] Eggshell
- [ ] Satin
- [ ] Semi gloss
- [ ] High gloss

Trim Color _____
- [ ] Flat
- [ ] Matte
- [ ] Eggshell
- [ ] Satin
- [ ] Semi gloss
- [ ] High gloss

Notes

Date _____

Job Name _____ ph # _____

Job Address _____

Paint Brand _____

Room Name

Wall Color _____
- ☐ Flat ☐ Satin
- ☐ Matte ☐ Semi gloss
- ☐ Eggshell ☐ High gloss

Ceiling Color _____
- ☐ Flat ☐ Satin
- ☐ Matte ☐ Semi gloss
- ☐ Eggshell ☐ High gloss

Trim Color _____
- ☐ Flat ☐ Satin
- ☐ Matte ☐ Semi gloss
- ☐ Eggshell ☐ High gloss

Notes

Room Name

Wall Color _____
- ☐ Flat ☐ Satin
- ☐ Matte ☐ Semi gloss
- ☐ Eggshell ☐ High gloss

Ceiling Color _____
- ☐ Flat ☐ Satin
- ☐ Matte ☐ Semi gloss
- ☐ Eggshell ☐ High gloss

Trim Color _____
- ☐ Flat ☐ Satin
- ☐ Matte ☐ Semi gloss
- ☐ Eggshell ☐ High gloss

Notes

Date _____

Job Name _____ ph # _____

Job Address _____

Paint Brand _____

Room Name

Wall Color _____
- [ ] Flat
- [ ] Matte
- [ ] Eggshell
- [ ] Satin
- [ ] Semi gloss
- [ ] High gloss

Ceiling Color _____
- [ ] Flat
- [ ] Matte
- [ ] Eggshell
- [ ] Satin
- [ ] Semi gloss
- [ ] High gloss

Trim Color _____
- [ ] Flat
- [ ] Matte
- [ ] Eggshell
- [ ] Satin
- [ ] Semi gloss
- [ ] High gloss

Notes

Room Name

Wall Color _____
- [ ] Flat
- [ ] Matte
- [ ] Eggshell
- [ ] Satin
- [ ] Semi gloss
- [ ] High gloss

Ceiling Color _____
- [ ] Flat
- [ ] Matte
- [ ] Eggshell
- [ ] Satin
- [ ] Semi gloss
- [ ] High gloss

Trim Color _____
- [ ] Flat
- [ ] Matte
- [ ] Eggshell
- [ ] Satin
- [ ] Semi gloss
- [ ] High gloss

Notes

Date _____

Job Name _____ ph # _____

Job Address _____

Paint Brand _____

Room Name _____

Wall Color _____
- ☐ Flat   ☐ Satin
- ☐ Matte   ☐ Semi gloss
- ☐ Eggshell ☐ High gloss

Ceiling Color _____
- ☐ Flat   ☐ Satin
- ☐ Matte   ☐ Semi gloss
- ☐ Eggshell ☐ High gloss

Trim Color _____
- ☐ Flat   ☐ Satin
- ☐ Matte   ☐ Semi gloss
- ☐ Eggshell ☐ High gloss

Notes

Room Name _____

Wall Color _____
- ☐ Flat   ☐ Satin
- ☐ Matte   ☐ Semi gloss
- ☐ Eggshell ☐ High gloss

Ceiling Color _____
- ☐ Flat   ☐ Satin
- ☐ Matte   ☐ Semi gloss
- ☐ Eggshell ☐ High gloss

Trim Color _____
- ☐ Flat   ☐ Satin
- ☐ Matte   ☐ Semi gloss
- ☐ Eggshell ☐ High gloss

Notes

Date _____

Job Name _____   ph # _____

Job Address _____

Paint Brand _____

Room Name

Wall Color	☐ Flat ☐ Matte ☐ Eggshell	☐ Satin ☐ Semi gloss ☐ High gloss
Ceiling Color	☐ Flat ☐ Matte ☐ Eggshell	☐ Satin ☐ Semi gloss ☐ High gloss
Trim Color	☐ Flat ☐ Matte ☐ Eggshell	☐ Satin ☐ Semi gloss ☐ High gloss

Notes

Room Name

Wall Color	☐ Flat ☐ Matte ☐ Eggshell	☐ Satin ☐ Semi gloss ☐ High gloss
Ceiling Color	☐ Flat ☐ Matte ☐ Eggshell	☐ Satin ☐ Semi gloss ☐ High gloss
Trim Color	☐ Flat ☐ Matte ☐ Eggshell	☐ Satin ☐ Semi gloss ☐ High gloss

Notes

Date _____

Job Name _____ ph # _____

Job Address _____

Paint Brand _____

Room Name _____

Wall Color _____
- [ ] Flat   [ ] Satin
- [ ] Matte   [ ] Semi gloss
- [ ] Eggshell   [ ] High gloss

Ceiling Color _____
- [ ] Flat   [ ] Satin
- [ ] Matte   [ ] Semi gloss
- [ ] Eggshell   [ ] High gloss

Trim Color _____
- [ ] Flat   [ ] Satin
- [ ] Matte   [ ] Semi gloss
- [ ] Eggshell   [ ] High gloss

Notes

Room Name _____

Wall Color _____
- [ ] Flat   [ ] Satin
- [ ] Matte   [ ] Semi gloss
- [ ] Eggshell   [ ] High gloss

Ceiling Color _____
- [ ] Flat   [ ] Satin
- [ ] Matte   [ ] Semi gloss
- [ ] Eggshell   [ ] High gloss

Trim Color _____
- [ ] Flat   [ ] Satin
- [ ] Matte   [ ] Semi gloss
- [ ] Eggshell   [ ] High gloss

Notes

Date

Job Name _____ ph # _____

Job Address _____

Paint Brand _____

Room Name

Wall Color _____
- ☐ Flat ☐ Satin
- ☐ Matte ☐ Semi gloss
- ☐ Eggshell ☐ High gloss

Ceiling Color _____
- ☐ Flat ☐ Satin
- ☐ Matte ☐ Semi gloss
- ☐ Eggshell ☐ High gloss

Trim Color _____
- ☐ Flat ☐ Satin
- ☐ Matte ☐ Semi gloss
- ☐ Eggshell ☐ High gloss

Notes

Room Name

Wall Color _____
- ☐ Flat ☐ Satin
- ☐ Matte ☐ Semi gloss
- ☐ Eggshell ☐ High gloss

Ceiling Color _____
- ☐ Flat ☐ Satin
- ☐ Matte ☐ Semi gloss
- ☐ Eggshell ☐ High gloss

Trim Color _____
- ☐ Flat ☐ Satin
- ☐ Matte ☐ Semi gloss
- ☐ Eggshell ☐ High gloss

Notes

Date _____

Job Name _____ ph # _____

Job Address _____

Paint Brand _____

Room Name _____

Wall Color _____
- ☐ Flat ☐ Satin
- ☐ Matte ☐ Semi gloss
- ☐ Eggshell ☐ High gloss

Ceiling Color _____
- ☐ Flat ☐ Satin
- ☐ Matte ☐ Semi gloss
- ☐ Eggshell ☐ High gloss

Trim Color _____
- ☐ Flat ☐ Satin
- ☐ Matte ☐ Semi gloss
- ☐ Eggshell ☐ High gloss

Notes

Room Name _____

Wall Color _____
- ☐ Flat ☐ Satin
- ☐ Matte ☐ Semi gloss
- ☐ Eggshell ☐ High gloss

Ceiling Color _____
- ☐ Flat ☐ Satin
- ☐ Matte ☐ Semi gloss
- ☐ Eggshell ☐ High gloss

Trim Color _____
- ☐ Flat ☐ Satin
- ☐ Matte ☐ Semi gloss
- ☐ Eggshell ☐ High gloss

Notes

Date _____

Job Name _____   ph # _____

Job Address _____

Paint Brand _____

Room Name _____

Wall Color _____
- [ ] Flat
- [ ] Matte
- [ ] Eggshell
- [ ] Satin
- [ ] Semi gloss
- [ ] High gloss

Ceiling Color _____
- [ ] Flat
- [ ] Matte
- [ ] Eggshell
- [ ] Satin
- [ ] Semi gloss
- [ ] High gloss

Trim Color _____
- [ ] Flat
- [ ] Matte
- [ ] Eggshell
- [ ] Satin
- [ ] Semi gloss
- [ ] High gloss

Notes

Room Name _____

Wall Color _____
- [ ] Flat
- [ ] Matte
- [ ] Eggshell
- [ ] Satin
- [ ] Semi gloss
- [ ] High gloss

Ceiling Color _____
- [ ] Flat
- [ ] Matte
- [ ] Eggshell
- [ ] Satin
- [ ] Semi gloss
- [ ] High gloss

Trim Color _____
- [ ] Flat
- [ ] Matte
- [ ] Eggshell
- [ ] Satin
- [ ] Semi gloss
- [ ] High gloss

Notes

Date _____

Job Name _____ ph # _____

Job Address _____

Paint Brand _____

Room Name _____

☐ Flat	☐ Satin
☐ Matte	☐ Semi gloss
☐ Eggshell	☐ High gloss

Wall Color _____

☐ Flat	☐ Satin
☐ Matte	☐ Semi gloss
☐ Eggshell	☐ High gloss

Ceiling Color _____

☐ Flat	☐ Satin
☐ Matte	☐ Semi gloss
☐ Eggshell	☐ High gloss

Trim Color _____

Notes

Room Name _____

☐ Flat	☐ Satin
☐ Matte	☐ Semi gloss
☐ Eggshell	☐ High gloss

Wall Color _____

☐ Flat	☐ Satin
☐ Matte	☐ Semi gloss
☐ Eggshell	☐ High gloss

Ceiling Color _____

☐ Flat	☐ Satin
☐ Matte	☐ Semi gloss
☐ Eggshell	☐ High gloss

Trim Color _____

Notes

Date _____

Job Name _____ ph # _____

Job Address _____

Paint Brand _____

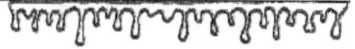

Room Name _____

Wall Color _____

☐ Flat	☐ Satin
☐ Matte	☐ Semi gloss
☐ Eggshell	☐ High gloss

Ceiling Color _____

☐ Flat	☐ Satin
☐ Matte	☐ Semi gloss
☐ Eggshell	☐ High gloss

Trim Color _____

☐ Flat	☐ Satin
☐ Matte	☐ Semi gloss
☐ Eggshell	☐ High gloss

Notes

Room Name _____

Wall Color _____

☐ Flat	☐ Satin
☐ Matte	☐ Semi gloss
☐ Eggshell	☐ High gloss

Ceiling Color _____

☐ Flat	☐ Satin
☐ Matte	☐ Semi gloss
☐ Eggshell	☐ High gloss

Trim Color _____

☐ Flat	☐ Satin
☐ Matte	☐ Semi gloss
☐ Eggshell	☐ High gloss

Notes

Date _____

Job Name _____   ph # _____

Job Address _____

Paint Brand _____

Room Name
_____

Wall Color _____
☐ Flat ☐ Satin
☐ Matte ☐ Semi gloss
☐ Eggshell ☐ High gloss

Ceiling Color _____
☐ Flat ☐ Satin
☐ Matte ☐ Semi gloss
☐ Eggshell ☐ High gloss

Trim Color _____
☐ Flat ☐ Satin
☐ Matte ☐ Semi gloss
☐ Eggshell ☐ High gloss

Notes

Room Name
_____

Wall Color _____
☐ Flat ☐ Satin
☐ Matte ☐ Semi gloss
☐ Eggshell ☐ High gloss

Ceiling Color _____
☐ Flat ☐ Satin
☐ Matte ☐ Semi gloss
☐ Eggshell ☐ High gloss

Trim Color _____
☐ Flat ☐ Satin
☐ Matte ☐ Semi gloss
☐ Eggshell ☐ High gloss

Notes

Date _____

Job Name _____ ph # _____

Job Address _____

Paint Brand _____

Room Name _____

Wall Color _____
- [ ] Flat
- [ ] Matte
- [ ] Eggshell
- [ ] Satin
- [ ] Semi gloss
- [ ] High gloss

Ceiling Color _____
- [ ] Flat
- [ ] Matte
- [ ] Eggshell
- [ ] Satin
- [ ] Semi gloss
- [ ] High gloss

Trim Color _____
- [ ] Flat
- [ ] Matte
- [ ] Eggshell
- [ ] Satin
- [ ] Semi gloss
- [ ] High gloss

Notes

Room Name _____

Wall Color _____
- [ ] Flat
- [ ] Matte
- [ ] Eggshell
- [ ] Satin
- [ ] Semi gloss
- [ ] High gloss

Ceiling Color _____
- [ ] Flat
- [ ] Matte
- [ ] Eggshell
- [ ] Satin
- [ ] Semi gloss
- [ ] High gloss

Trim Color _____
- [ ] Flat
- [ ] Matte
- [ ] Eggshell
- [ ] Satin
- [ ] Semi gloss
- [ ] High gloss

Notes

Date _____

Job Name _____ ph # _____

Job Address _____

Paint Brand _____

Room Name
_____

Wall Color _____
- ☐ Flat   ☐ Satin
- ☐ Matte   ☐ Semi gloss
- ☐ Eggshell   ☐ High gloss

Ceiling Color _____
- ☐ Flat   ☐ Satin
- ☐ Matte   ☐ Semi gloss
- ☐ Eggshell   ☐ High gloss

Trim Color _____
- ☐ Flat   ☐ Satin
- ☐ Matte   ☐ Semi gloss
- ☐ Eggshell   ☐ High gloss

Notes

Room Name
_____

Wall Color _____
- ☐ Flat   ☐ Satin
- ☐ Matte   ☐ Semi gloss
- ☐ Eggshell   ☐ High gloss

Ceiling Color _____
- ☐ Flat   ☐ Satin
- ☐ Matte   ☐ Semi gloss
- ☐ Eggshell   ☐ High gloss

Trim Color _____
- ☐ Flat   ☐ Satin
- ☐ Matte   ☐ Semi gloss
- ☐ Eggshell   ☐ High gloss

Notes

Date _____

Job Name _____ ph # _____

Job Address _____

Paint Brand _____

Room Name _____

Wall Color _____
- [ ] Flat
- [ ] Matte
- [ ] Eggshell
- [ ] Satin
- [ ] Semi gloss
- [ ] High gloss

Ceiling Color _____
- [ ] Flat
- [ ] Matte
- [ ] Eggshell
- [ ] Satin
- [ ] Semi gloss
- [ ] High gloss

Trim Color _____
- [ ] Flat
- [ ] Matte
- [ ] Eggshell
- [ ] Satin
- [ ] Semi gloss
- [ ] High gloss

Notes

Room Name _____

Wall Color _____
- [ ] Flat
- [ ] Matte
- [ ] Eggshell
- [ ] Satin
- [ ] Semi gloss
- [ ] High gloss

Ceiling Color _____
- [ ] Flat
- [ ] Matte
- [ ] Eggshell
- [ ] Satin
- [ ] Semi gloss
- [ ] High gloss

Trim Color _____
- [ ] Flat
- [ ] Matte
- [ ] Eggshell
- [ ] Satin
- [ ] Semi gloss
- [ ] High gloss

Notes

Date _____

Job Name _____ ph # _____

Job Address _____

Paint Brand _____

Room Name _____

Wall Color _____
- ☐ Flat   ☐ Satin
- ☐ Matte   ☐ Semi gloss
- ☐ Eggshell   ☐ High gloss

Ceiling Color _____
- ☐ Flat   ☐ Satin
- ☐ Matte   ☐ Semi gloss
- ☐ Eggshell   ☐ High gloss

Trim Color _____
- ☐ Flat   ☐ Satin
- ☐ Matte   ☐ Semi gloss
- ☐ Eggshell   ☐ High gloss

Notes

Room Name _____

Wall Color _____
- ☐ Flat   ☐ Satin
- ☐ Matte   ☐ Semi gloss
- ☐ Eggshell   ☐ High gloss

Ceiling Color _____
- ☐ Flat   ☐ Satin
- ☐ Matte   ☐ Semi gloss
- ☐ Eggshell   ☐ High gloss

Trim Color _____
- ☐ Flat   ☐ Satin
- ☐ Matte   ☐ Semi gloss
- ☐ Eggshell   ☐ High gloss

Notes

Date _____

Job Name _____ ph # _____

Job Address _____

Paint Brand _____

Room Name _____

☐ Flat	☐ Satin
☐ Matte	☐ Semi gloss
☐ Eggshell	☐ High gloss

Wall Color _____

☐ Flat	☐ Satin
☐ Matte	☐ Semi gloss
☐ Eggshell	☐ High gloss

Ceiling Color _____

☐ Flat	☐ Satin
☐ Matte	☐ Semi gloss
☐ Eggshell	☐ High gloss

Trim Color _____

Notes

Room Name _____

☐ Flat	☐ Satin
☐ Matte	☐ Semi gloss
☐ Eggshell	☐ High gloss

Wall Color _____

☐ Flat	☐ Satin
☐ Matte	☐ Semi gloss
☐ Eggshell	☐ High gloss

Ceiling Color _____

☐ Flat	☐ Satin
☐ Matte	☐ Semi gloss
☐ Eggshell	☐ High gloss

Trim Color _____

Notes

Date _____

Job Name _____ ph # _____

Job Address _____

Paint Brand _____

Room Name _____

☐ Flat	☐ Satin
☐ Matte	☐ Semi gloss

Wall Color _____ ☐ Eggshell ☐ High gloss

☐ Flat	☐ Satin
☐ Matte	☐ Semi gloss

Ceiling Color _____ ☐ Eggshell ☐ High gloss

☐ Flat	☐ Satin
☐ Matte	☐ Semi gloss

Trim Color _____ ☐ Eggshell ☐ High gloss

Notes

Room Name _____

☐ Flat	☐ Satin
☐ Matte	☐ Semi gloss

Wall Color _____ ☐ Eggshell ☐ High gloss

☐ Flat	☐ Satin
☐ Matte	☐ Semi gloss

Ceiling Color _____ ☐ Eggshell ☐ High gloss

☐ Flat	☐ Satin
☐ Matte	☐ Semi gloss

Trim Color _____ ☐ Eggshell ☐ High gloss

Notes

Date _____

Job Name _____ ph # _____

Job Address _____

Paint Brand _____

Room Name _____

Wall Color _____
- ☐ Flat ☐ Satin
- ☐ Matte ☐ Semi gloss
- ☐ Eggshell ☐ High gloss

Ceiling Color _____
- ☐ Flat ☐ Satin
- ☐ Matte ☐ Semi gloss
- ☐ Eggshell ☐ High gloss

Trim Color _____
- ☐ Flat ☐ Satin
- ☐ Matte ☐ Semi gloss
- ☐ Eggshell ☐ High gloss

Notes

Room Name _____

Wall Color _____
- ☐ Flat ☐ Satin
- ☐ Matte ☐ Semi gloss
- ☐ Eggshell ☐ High gloss

Ceiling Color _____
- ☐ Flat ☐ Satin
- ☐ Matte ☐ Semi gloss
- ☐ Eggshell ☐ High gloss

Trim Color _____
- ☐ Flat ☐ Satin
- ☐ Matte ☐ Semi gloss
- ☐ Eggshell ☐ High gloss

Notes

Date _____

Job Name _____ ph # _____

Job Address _____

Paint Brand _____

Room Name

_____

Wall Color _____
- [ ] Flat
- [ ] Matte
- [ ] Eggshell
- [ ] Satin
- [ ] Semi gloss
- [ ] High gloss

Ceiling Color _____
- [ ] Flat
- [ ] Matte
- [ ] Eggshell
- [ ] Satin
- [ ] Semi gloss
- [ ] High gloss

Trim Color _____
- [ ] Flat
- [ ] Matte
- [ ] Eggshell
- [ ] Satin
- [ ] Semi gloss
- [ ] High gloss

Notes

Room Name

_____

Wall Color _____
- [ ] Flat
- [ ] Matte
- [ ] Eggshell
- [ ] Satin
- [ ] Semi gloss
- [ ] High gloss

Ceiling Color _____
- [ ] Flat
- [ ] Matte
- [ ] Eggshell
- [ ] Satin
- [ ] Semi gloss
- [ ] High gloss

Trim Color _____
- [ ] Flat
- [ ] Matte
- [ ] Eggshell
- [ ] Satin
- [ ] Semi gloss
- [ ] High gloss

Notes

Date _____

Job Name _____   ph # _____

Job Address _____

Paint Brand _____

Room Name _____

Wall Color _____
- ☐ Flat   ☐ Satin
- ☐ Matte   ☐ Semi gloss
- ☐ Eggshell ☐ High gloss

Ceiling Color _____
- ☐ Flat   ☐ Satin
- ☐ Matte   ☐ Semi gloss
- ☐ Eggshell ☐ High gloss

Trim Color _____
- ☐ Flat   ☐ Satin
- ☐ Matte   ☐ Semi gloss
- ☐ Eggshell ☐ High gloss

Notes
_____

Room Name _____

Wall Color _____
- ☐ Flat   ☐ Satin
- ☐ Matte   ☐ Semi gloss
- ☐ Eggshell ☐ High gloss

Ceiling Color _____
- ☐ Flat   ☐ Satin
- ☐ Matte   ☐ Semi gloss
- ☐ Eggshell ☐ High gloss

Trim Color _____
- ☐ Flat   ☐ Satin
- ☐ Matte   ☐ Semi gloss
- ☐ Eggshell ☐ High gloss

Notes
_____

Date _____

Job Name _____ ph # _____

Job Address _____

Paint Brand _____

Room Name

Wall Color _____
- ☐ Flat ☐ Satin
- ☐ Matte ☐ Semi gloss
- ☐ Eggshell ☐ High gloss

Ceiling Color _____
- ☐ Flat ☐ Satin
- ☐ Matte ☐ Semi gloss
- ☐ Eggshell ☐ High gloss

Trim Color _____
- ☐ Flat ☐ Satin
- ☐ Matte ☐ Semi gloss
- ☐ Eggshell ☐ High gloss

Notes

Room Name

Wall Color _____
- ☐ Flat ☐ Satin
- ☐ Matte ☐ Semi gloss
- ☐ Eggshell ☐ High gloss

Ceiling Color _____
- ☐ Flat ☐ Satin
- ☐ Matte ☐ Semi gloss
- ☐ Eggshell ☐ High gloss

Trim Color _____
- ☐ Flat ☐ Satin
- ☐ Matte ☐ Semi gloss
- ☐ Eggshell ☐ High gloss

Notes

Date _____

Job Name _____ ph # _____

Job Address _____

Paint Brand _____

Room Name _____

Wall Color _____
☐ Flat ☐ Satin
☐ Matte ☐ Semi gloss
☐ Eggshell ☐ High gloss

Ceiling Color _____
☐ Flat ☐ Satin
☐ Matte ☐ Semi gloss
☐ Eggshell ☐ High gloss

Trim Color _____
☐ Flat ☐ Satin
☐ Matte ☐ Semi gloss
☐ Eggshell ☐ High gloss

Notes

Room Name _____

Wall Color _____
☐ Flat ☐ Satin
☐ Matte ☐ Semi gloss
☐ Eggshell ☐ High gloss

Ceiling Color _____
☐ Flat ☐ Satin
☐ Matte ☐ Semi gloss
☐ Eggshell ☐ High gloss

Trim Color _____
☐ Flat ☐ Satin
☐ Matte ☐ Semi gloss
☐ Eggshell ☐ High gloss

Notes

Date _____

Job Name _____ ph # _____

Job Address _____

Paint Brand _____

Room Name

Wall Color _____

☐ Flat	☐ Satin
☐ Matte	☐ Semi gloss
☐ Eggshell	☐ High gloss

Ceiling Color _____

☐ Flat	☐ Satin
☐ Matte	☐ Semi gloss
☐ Eggshell	☐ High gloss

Trim Color _____

☐ Flat	☐ Satin
☐ Matte	☐ Semi gloss
☐ Eggshell	☐ High gloss

Notes

Room Name

Wall Color _____

☐ Flat	☐ Satin
☐ Matte	☐ Semi gloss
☐ Eggshell	☐ High gloss

Ceiling Color _____

☐ Flat	☐ Satin
☐ Matte	☐ Semi gloss
☐ Eggshell	☐ High gloss

Trim Color _____

☐ Flat	☐ Satin
☐ Matte	☐ Semi gloss
☐ Eggshell	☐ High gloss

Notes

Date _____

Job Name _____ ph # _____

Job Address _____

Paint Brand _____

Room Name

Wall Color _____

☐ Flat   ☐ Satin
☐ Matte   ☐ Semi gloss
☐ Eggshell   ☐ High gloss

Ceiling Color _____

☐ Flat   ☐ Satin
☐ Matte   ☐ Semi gloss
☐ Eggshell   ☐ High gloss

Trim Color _____

☐ Flat   ☐ Satin
☐ Matte   ☐ Semi gloss
☐ Eggshell   ☐ High gloss

Notes

Room Name

Wall Color _____

☐ Flat   ☐ Satin
☐ Matte   ☐ Semi gloss
☐ Eggshell   ☐ High gloss

Ceiling Color _____

☐ Flat   ☐ Satin
☐ Matte   ☐ Semi gloss
☐ Eggshell   ☐ High gloss

Trim Color _____

☐ Flat   ☐ Satin
☐ Matte   ☐ Semi gloss
☐ Eggshell   ☐ High gloss

Notes

Date _____

Job Name _____   ph # _____

Job Address _____

Paint Brand _____

Room Name
_____

Wall Color _____

☐ Flat	☐ Satin
☐ Matte	☐ Semi gloss
☐ Eggshell	☐ High gloss

Ceiling Color _____

☐ Flat	☐ Satin
☐ Matte	☐ Semi gloss
☐ Eggshell	☐ High gloss

Trim Color _____

☐ Flat	☐ Satin
☐ Matte	☐ Semi gloss
☐ Eggshell	☐ High gloss

Notes

Room Name
_____

Wall Color _____

☐ Flat	☐ Satin
☐ Matte	☐ Semi gloss
☐ Eggshell	☐ High gloss

Ceiling Color _____

☐ Flat	☐ Satin
☐ Matte	☐ Semi gloss
☐ Eggshell	☐ High gloss

Trim Color _____

☐ Flat	☐ Satin
☐ Matte	☐ Semi gloss
☐ Eggshell	☐ High gloss

Notes

Date _____

Job Name _____ ph # _____

Job Address _____

Paint Brand _____

Room Name

Wall Color	☐ Flat ☐ Matte ☐ Eggshell	☐ Satin ☐ Semi gloss ☐ High gloss
Ceiling Color	☐ Flat ☐ Matte ☐ Eggshell	☐ Satin ☐ Semi gloss ☐ High gloss
Trim Color	☐ Flat ☐ Matte ☐ Eggshell	☐ Satin ☐ Semi gloss ☐ High gloss

Notes

Room Name

Wall Color	☐ Flat ☐ Matte ☐ Eggshell	☐ Satin ☐ Semi gloss ☐ High gloss
Ceiling Color	☐ Flat ☐ Matte ☐ Eggshell	☐ Satin ☐ Semi gloss ☐ High gloss
Trim Color	☐ Flat ☐ Matte ☐ Eggshell	☐ Satin ☐ Semi gloss ☐ High gloss

Notes

Date _____

Job Name _____   ph # _____

Job Address _____

Paint Brand _____

Room Name _____

Wall Color _____
- [ ] Flat [ ] Satin
- [ ] Matte [ ] Semi gloss
- [ ] Eggshell [ ] High gloss

Ceiling Color _____
- [ ] Flat [ ] Satin
- [ ] Matte [ ] Semi gloss
- [ ] Eggshell [ ] High gloss

Trim Color _____
- [ ] Flat [ ] Satin
- [ ] Matte [ ] Semi gloss
- [ ] Eggshell [ ] High gloss

Notes

Room Name _____

Wall Color _____
- [ ] Flat [ ] Satin
- [ ] Matte [ ] Semi gloss
- [ ] Eggshell [ ] High gloss

Ceiling Color _____
- [ ] Flat [ ] Satin
- [ ] Matte [ ] Semi gloss
- [ ] Eggshell [ ] High gloss

Trim Color _____
- [ ] Flat [ ] Satin
- [ ] Matte [ ] Semi gloss
- [ ] Eggshell [ ] High gloss

Notes

Date _____

Job Name _____ ph # _____

Job Address _____

Paint Brand _____

Room Name

Wall Color _____
- ☐ Flat ☐ Satin
- ☐ Matte ☐ Semi gloss
- ☐ Eggshell ☐ High gloss

Ceiling Color _____
- ☐ Flat ☐ Satin
- ☐ Matte ☐ Semi gloss
- ☐ Eggshell ☐ High gloss

Trim Color _____
- ☐ Flat ☐ Satin
- ☐ Matte ☐ Semi gloss
- ☐ Eggshell ☐ High gloss

Notes

Room Name

Wall Color _____
- ☐ Flat ☐ Satin
- ☐ Matte ☐ Semi gloss
- ☐ Eggshell ☐ High gloss

Ceiling Color _____
- ☐ Flat ☐ Satin
- ☐ Matte ☐ Semi gloss
- ☐ Eggshell ☐ High gloss

Trim Color _____
- ☐ Flat ☐ Satin
- ☐ Matte ☐ Semi gloss
- ☐ Eggshell ☐ High gloss

Notes

Date _____

Job Name _____ ph # _____

Job Address _____

Paint Brand _____

Room Name _____

Wall Color _____
☐ Flat ☐ Satin
☐ Matte ☐ Semi gloss
☐ Eggshell ☐ High gloss

Ceiling Color _____
☐ Flat ☐ Satin
☐ Matte ☐ Semi gloss
☐ Eggshell ☐ High gloss

Trim Color _____
☐ Flat ☐ Satin
☐ Matte ☐ Semi gloss
☐ Eggshell ☐ High gloss

Notes

Room Name _____

Wall Color _____
☐ Flat ☐ Satin
☐ Matte ☐ Semi gloss
☐ Eggshell ☐ High gloss

Ceiling Color _____
☐ Flat ☐ Satin
☐ Matte ☐ Semi gloss
☐ Eggshell ☐ High gloss

Trim Color _____
☐ Flat ☐ Satin
☐ Matte ☐ Semi gloss
☐ Eggshell ☐ High gloss

Notes

Date _____

Job Name _____ ph # _____

Job Address _____

Paint Brand _____

Room Name _____

Wall Color _____
- ☐ Flat ☐ Satin
- ☐ Matte ☐ Semi gloss
- ☐ Eggshell ☐ High gloss

Ceiling Color _____
- ☐ Flat ☐ Satin
- ☐ Matte ☐ Semi gloss
- ☐ Eggshell ☐ High gloss

Trim Color _____
- ☐ Flat ☐ Satin
- ☐ Matte ☐ Semi gloss
- ☐ Eggshell ☐ High gloss

Notes

Room Name _____

Wall Color _____
- ☐ Flat ☐ Satin
- ☐ Matte ☐ Semi gloss
- ☐ Eggshell ☐ High gloss

Ceiling Color _____
- ☐ Flat ☐ Satin
- ☐ Matte ☐ Semi gloss
- ☐ Eggshell ☐ High gloss

Trim Color _____
- ☐ Flat ☐ Satin
- ☐ Matte ☐ Semi gloss
- ☐ Eggshell ☐ High gloss

Notes

Date _____

Job Name _____ ph # _____

Job Address _____

Paint Brand _____

Room Name
_____

☐ Flat	☐ Satin
☐ Matte	☐ Semi gloss
☐ Eggshell	☐ High gloss

Wall Color _____

☐ Flat	☐ Satin
☐ Matte	☐ Semi gloss
☐ Eggshell	☐ High gloss

Ceiling Color _____

☐ Flat	☐ Satin
☐ Matte	☐ Semi gloss
☐ Eggshell	☐ High gloss

Trim Color _____

Notes

Room Name
_____

☐ Flat	☐ Satin
☐ Matte	☐ Semi gloss
☐ Eggshell	☐ High gloss

Wall Color _____

☐ Flat	☐ Satin
☐ Matte	☐ Semi gloss
☐ Eggshell	☐ High gloss

Ceiling Color _____

☐ Flat	☐ Satin
☐ Matte	☐ Semi gloss
☐ Eggshell	☐ High gloss

Trim Color _____

Notes

Date _____

Job Name _____ ph # _____

Job Address _____

Paint Brand _____

Room Name _____

Wall Color _____
- ☐ Flat ☐ Satin
- ☐ Matte ☐ Semi gloss
- ☐ Eggshell ☐ High gloss

Ceiling Color _____
- ☐ Flat ☐ Satin
- ☐ Matte ☐ Semi gloss
- ☐ Eggshell ☐ High gloss

Trim Color _____
- ☐ Flat ☐ Satin
- ☐ Matte ☐ Semi gloss
- ☐ Eggshell ☐ High gloss

Notes

Room Name _____

Wall Color _____
- ☐ Flat ☐ Satin
- ☐ Matte ☐ Semi gloss
- ☐ Eggshell ☐ High gloss

Ceiling Color _____
- ☐ Flat ☐ Satin
- ☐ Matte ☐ Semi gloss
- ☐ Eggshell ☐ High gloss

Trim Color _____
- ☐ Flat ☐ Satin
- ☐ Matte ☐ Semi gloss
- ☐ Eggshell ☐ High gloss

Notes

Date _____

Job Name _____   ph # _____

Job Address _____

Paint Brand _____

Room Name _____

Wall Color _____
☐ Flat   ☐ Satin
☐ Matte   ☐ Semi gloss
☐ Eggshell ☐ High gloss

Ceiling Color _____
☐ Flat   ☐ Satin
☐ Matte   ☐ Semi gloss
☐ Eggshell ☐ High gloss

Trim Color _____
☐ Flat   ☐ Satin
☐ Matte   ☐ Semi gloss
☐ Eggshell ☐ High gloss

Notes

Room Name _____

Wall Color _____
☐ Flat   ☐ Satin
☐ Matte   ☐ Semi gloss
☐ Eggshell ☐ High gloss

Ceiling Color _____
☐ Flat   ☐ Satin
☐ Matte   ☐ Semi gloss
☐ Eggshell ☐ High gloss

Trim Color _____
☐ Flat   ☐ Satin
☐ Matte   ☐ Semi gloss
☐ Eggshell ☐ High gloss

Notes

Date _____

Job Name _____ ph # _____

Job Address _____

Paint Brand _____

Room Name _____

	Flat	Satin
Wall Color	☐ Flat	☐ Satin
	☐ Matte	☐ Semi gloss
	☐ Eggshell	☐ High gloss
Ceiling Color	☐ Flat	☐ Satin
	☐ Matte	☐ Semi gloss
	☐ Eggshell	☐ High gloss
Trim Color	☐ Flat	☐ Satin
	☐ Matte	☐ Semi gloss
	☐ Eggshell	☐ High gloss

Notes

Room Name _____

	Flat	Satin
Wall Color	☐ Flat	☐ Satin
	☐ Matte	☐ Semi gloss
	☐ Eggshell	☐ High gloss
Ceiling Color	☐ Flat	☐ Satin
	☐ Matte	☐ Semi gloss
	☐ Eggshell	☐ High gloss
Trim Color	☐ Flat	☐ Satin
	☐ Matte	☐ Semi gloss
	☐ Eggshell	☐ High gloss

Notes

Date _____

Job Name _____ ph # _____

Job Address _____

Paint Brand _____

Room Name _____

☐ Flat	☐ Satin
☐ Matte	☐ Semi gloss
☐ Eggshell	☐ High gloss

Wall Color _____

☐ Flat	☐ Satin
☐ Matte	☐ Semi gloss
☐ Eggshell	☐ High gloss

Ceiling Color _____

☐ Flat	☐ Satin
☐ Matte	☐ Semi gloss
☐ Eggshell	☐ High gloss

Trim Color _____

Notes

Room Name _____

☐ Flat	☐ Satin
☐ Matte	☐ Semi gloss
☐ Eggshell	☐ High gloss

Wall Color _____

☐ Flat	☐ Satin
☐ Matte	☐ Semi gloss
☐ Eggshell	☐ High gloss

Ceiling Color _____

☐ Flat	☐ Satin
☐ Matte	☐ Semi gloss
☐ Eggshell	☐ High gloss

Trim Color _____

Notes

Date _____

Job Name _____ ph # _____

Job Address _____

Paint Brand _____

Room Name _____

Wall Color _____
- [ ] Flat
- [ ] Matte
- [ ] Eggshell
- [ ] Satin
- [ ] Semi gloss
- [ ] High gloss

Ceiling Color _____
- [ ] Flat
- [ ] Matte
- [ ] Eggshell
- [ ] Satin
- [ ] Semi gloss
- [ ] High gloss

Trim Color _____
- [ ] Flat
- [ ] Matte
- [ ] Eggshell
- [ ] Satin
- [ ] Semi gloss
- [ ] High gloss

Notes

Room Name _____

Wall Color _____
- [ ] Flat
- [ ] Matte
- [ ] Eggshell
- [ ] Satin
- [ ] Semi gloss
- [ ] High gloss

Ceiling Color _____
- [ ] Flat
- [ ] Matte
- [ ] Eggshell
- [ ] Satin
- [ ] Semi gloss
- [ ] High gloss

Trim Color _____
- [ ] Flat
- [ ] Matte
- [ ] Eggshell
- [ ] Satin
- [ ] Semi gloss
- [ ] High gloss

Notes

Date _____

Job Name _____   ph # _____

Job Address _____

Paint Brand _____

Room Name
_____

☐ Flat	☐ Satin
☐ Matte	☐ Semi gloss
☐ Eggshell	☐ High gloss

Wall Color _____

☐ Flat	☐ Satin
☐ Matte	☐ Semi gloss
☐ Eggshell	☐ High gloss

Ceiling Color _____

☐ Flat	☐ Satin
☐ Matte	☐ Semi gloss
☐ Eggshell	☐ High gloss

Trim Color _____

Notes

Room Name
_____

☐ Flat	☐ Satin
☐ Matte	☐ Semi gloss
☐ Eggshell	☐ High gloss

Wall Color _____

☐ Flat	☐ Satin
☐ Matte	☐ Semi gloss
☐ Eggshell	☐ High gloss

Ceiling Color _____

☐ Flat	☐ Satin
☐ Matte	☐ Semi gloss
☐ Eggshell	☐ High gloss

Trim Color _____

Notes

Date _____

Job Name _____ ph # _____

Job Address _____

Paint Brand _____

Room Name _____

Wall Color _____
- ☐ Flat ☐ Satin
- ☐ Matte ☐ Semi gloss
- ☐ Eggshell ☐ High gloss

Ceiling Color _____
- ☐ Flat ☐ Satin
- ☐ Matte ☐ Semi gloss
- ☐ Eggshell ☐ High gloss

Trim Color _____
- ☐ Flat ☐ Satin
- ☐ Matte ☐ Semi gloss
- ☐ Eggshell ☐ High gloss

Notes

Room Name _____

Wall Color _____
- ☐ Flat ☐ Satin
- ☐ Matte ☐ Semi gloss
- ☐ Eggshell ☐ High gloss

Ceiling Color _____
- ☐ Flat ☐ Satin
- ☐ Matte ☐ Semi gloss
- ☐ Eggshell ☐ High gloss

Trim Color _____
- ☐ Flat ☐ Satin
- ☐ Matte ☐ Semi gloss
- ☐ Eggshell ☐ High gloss

Notes

Date _____

Job Name _____ ph # _____

Job Address _____

Paint Brand _____

Room Name

Wall Color _____

- ☐ Flat ☐ Satin
- ☐ Matte ☐ Semi gloss
- ☐ Eggshell ☐ High gloss

Ceiling Color _____

- ☐ Flat ☐ Satin
- ☐ Matte ☐ Semi gloss
- ☐ Eggshell ☐ High gloss

Trim Color _____

- ☐ Flat ☐ Satin
- ☐ Matte ☐ Semi gloss
- ☐ Eggshell ☐ High gloss

Notes

Room Name

Wall Color _____

- ☐ Flat ☐ Satin
- ☐ Matte ☐ Semi gloss
- ☐ Eggshell ☐ High gloss

Ceiling Color _____

- ☐ Flat ☐ Satin
- ☐ Matte ☐ Semi gloss
- ☐ Eggshell ☐ High gloss

Trim Color _____

- ☐ Flat ☐ Satin
- ☐ Matte ☐ Semi gloss
- ☐ Eggshell ☐ High gloss

Notes

Date _____

Job Name _____   ph # _____

Job Address _____

Paint Brand _____

Room Name _____

Wall Color _____

☐ Flat ☐ Satin
☐ Matte ☐ Semi gloss
☐ Eggshell ☐ High gloss

Ceiling Color _____

☐ Flat ☐ Satin
☐ Matte ☐ Semi gloss
☐ Eggshell ☐ High gloss

Trim Color _____

☐ Flat ☐ Satin
☐ Matte ☐ Semi gloss
☐ Eggshell ☐ High gloss

Notes

Room Name _____

Wall Color _____

☐ Flat ☐ Satin
☐ Matte ☐ Semi gloss
☐ Eggshell ☐ High gloss

Ceiling Color _____

☐ Flat ☐ Satin
☐ Matte ☐ Semi gloss
☐ Eggshell ☐ High gloss

Trim Color _____

☐ Flat ☐ Satin
☐ Matte ☐ Semi gloss
☐ Eggshell ☐ High gloss

Notes

Date _____

Job Name _____   ph # _____

Job Address _____

Paint Brand _____

Room Name
_____

Wall Color	☐ Flat ☐ Matte ☐ Eggshell	☐ Satin ☐ Semi gloss ☐ High gloss
Ceiling Color	☐ Flat ☐ Matte ☐ Eggshell	☐ Satin ☐ Semi gloss ☐ High gloss
Trim Color	☐ Flat ☐ Matte ☐ Eggshell	☐ Satin ☐ Semi gloss ☐ High gloss

Notes

Room Name
_____

Wall Color	☐ Flat ☐ Matte ☐ Eggshell	☐ Satin ☐ Semi gloss ☐ High gloss
Ceiling Color	☐ Flat ☐ Matte ☐ Eggshell	☐ Satin ☐ Semi gloss ☐ High gloss
Trim Color	☐ Flat ☐ Matte ☐ Eggshell	☐ Satin ☐ Semi gloss ☐ High gloss

Notes

Date _____

Job Name _____ ph # _____

Job Address _____

Paint Brand _____

Room Name

Wall Color _____
☐ Flat ☐ Satin
☐ Matte ☐ Semi gloss
☐ Eggshell ☐ High gloss

Ceiling Color _____
☐ Flat ☐ Satin
☐ Matte ☐ Semi gloss
☐ Eggshell ☐ High gloss

Trim Color _____
☐ Flat ☐ Satin
☐ Matte ☐ Semi gloss
☐ Eggshell ☐ High gloss

Notes

Room Name

Wall Color _____
☐ Flat ☐ Satin
☐ Matte ☐ Semi gloss
☐ Eggshell ☐ High gloss

Ceiling Color _____
☐ Flat ☐ Satin
☐ Matte ☐ Semi gloss
☐ Eggshell ☐ High gloss

Trim Color _____
☐ Flat ☐ Satin
☐ Matte ☐ Semi gloss
☐ Eggshell ☐ High gloss

Notes

Date _____

Job Name _____   ph # _____

Job Address _____

Paint Brand _____

Room Name
_____

Wall Color _____

☐ Flat	☐ Satin
☐ Matte	☐ Semi gloss
☐ Eggshell	☐ High gloss

Ceiling Color _____

☐ Flat	☐ Satin
☐ Matte	☐ Semi gloss
☐ Eggshell	☐ High gloss

Trim Color _____

☐ Flat	☐ Satin
☐ Matte	☐ Semi gloss
☐ Eggshell	☐ High gloss

Notes

Room Name
_____

Wall Color _____

☐ Flat	☐ Satin
☐ Matte	☐ Semi gloss
☐ Eggshell	☐ High gloss

Ceiling Color _____

☐ Flat	☐ Satin
☐ Matte	☐ Semi gloss
☐ Eggshell	☐ High gloss

Trim Color _____

☐ Flat	☐ Satin
☐ Matte	☐ Semi gloss
☐ Eggshell	☐ High gloss

Notes

Date _____

Job Name _____ ph # _____

Job Address _____

Paint Brand _____

Room Name _____

Wall Color _____
- ☐ Flat   ☐ Satin
- ☐ Matte   ☐ Semi gloss
- ☐ Eggshell   ☐ High gloss

Ceiling Color _____
- ☐ Flat   ☐ Satin
- ☐ Matte   ☐ Semi gloss
- ☐ Eggshell   ☐ High gloss

Trim Color _____
- ☐ Flat   ☐ Satin
- ☐ Matte   ☐ Semi gloss
- ☐ Eggshell   ☐ High gloss

Notes

Room Name _____

Wall Color _____
- ☐ Flat   ☐ Satin
- ☐ Matte   ☐ Semi gloss
- ☐ Eggshell   ☐ High gloss

Ceiling Color _____
- ☐ Flat   ☐ Satin
- ☐ Matte   ☐ Semi gloss
- ☐ Eggshell   ☐ High gloss

Trim Color _____
- ☐ Flat   ☐ Satin
- ☐ Matte   ☐ Semi gloss
- ☐ Eggshell   ☐ High gloss

Notes

Date _____

Job Name _____ ph # _____

Job Address _____

Paint Brand _____

Room Name _____

Wall Color _____	☐ Flat ☐ Matte ☐ Eggshell	☐ Satin ☐ Semi gloss ☐ High gloss
Ceiling Color _____	☐ Flat ☐ Matte ☐ Eggshell	☐ Satin ☐ Semi gloss ☐ High gloss
Trim Color _____	☐ Flat ☐ Matte ☐ Eggshell	☐ Satin ☐ Semi gloss ☐ High gloss

Notes

Room Name _____

Wall Color _____	☐ Flat ☐ Matte ☐ Eggshell	☐ Satin ☐ Semi gloss ☐ High gloss
Ceiling Color _____	☐ Flat ☐ Matte ☐ Eggshell	☐ Satin ☐ Semi gloss ☐ High gloss
Trim Color _____	☐ Flat ☐ Matte ☐ Eggshell	☐ Satin ☐ Semi gloss ☐ High gloss

Notes

Date _____

Job Name _____   ph # _____

Job Address _____

Paint Brand _____

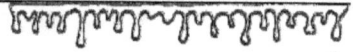

Room Name _____

Wall Color _____
☐ Flat ☐ Satin
☐ Matte ☐ Semi gloss
☐ Eggshell ☐ High gloss

Ceiling Color _____
☐ Flat ☐ Satin
☐ Matte ☐ Semi gloss
☐ Eggshell ☐ High gloss

Trim Color _____
☐ Flat ☐ Satin
☐ Matte ☐ Semi gloss
☐ Eggshell ☐ High gloss

Notes

Room Name _____

Wall Color _____
☐ Flat ☐ Satin
☐ Matte ☐ Semi gloss
☐ Eggshell ☐ High gloss

Ceiling Color _____
☐ Flat ☐ Satin
☐ Matte ☐ Semi gloss
☐ Eggshell ☐ High gloss

Trim Color _____
☐ Flat ☐ Satin
☐ Matte ☐ Semi gloss
☐ Eggshell ☐ High gloss

Notes

Date _____

Job Name _____ ph # _____

Job Address _____

Paint Brand _____

Room Name _____

Wall Color _____
- ☐ Flat ☐ Satin
- ☐ Matte ☐ Semi gloss
- ☐ Eggshell ☐ High gloss

Ceiling Color _____
- ☐ Flat ☐ Satin
- ☐ Matte ☐ Semi gloss
- ☐ Eggshell ☐ High gloss

Trim Color _____
- ☐ Flat ☐ Satin
- ☐ Matte ☐ Semi gloss
- ☐ Eggshell ☐ High gloss

Notes

Room Name _____

Wall Color _____
- ☐ Flat ☐ Satin
- ☐ Matte ☐ Semi gloss
- ☐ Eggshell ☐ High gloss

Ceiling Color _____
- ☐ Flat ☐ Satin
- ☐ Matte ☐ Semi gloss
- ☐ Eggshell ☐ High gloss

Trim Color _____
- ☐ Flat ☐ Satin
- ☐ Matte ☐ Semi gloss
- ☐ Eggshell ☐ High gloss

Notes

Date _____

Job Name _____ ph # _____

Job Address _____

Paint Brand _____

Room Name _____

Wall Color _____
- ☐ Flat ☐ Satin
- ☐ Matte ☐ Semi gloss
- ☐ Eggshell ☐ High gloss

Ceiling Color _____
- ☐ Flat ☐ Satin
- ☐ Matte ☐ Semi gloss
- ☐ Eggshell ☐ High gloss

Trim Color _____
- ☐ Flat ☐ Satin
- ☐ Matte ☐ Semi gloss
- ☐ Eggshell ☐ High gloss

Notes

Room Name _____

Wall Color _____
- ☐ Flat ☐ Satin
- ☐ Matte ☐ Semi gloss
- ☐ Eggshell ☐ High gloss

Ceiling Color _____
- ☐ Flat ☐ Satin
- ☐ Matte ☐ Semi gloss
- ☐ Eggshell ☐ High gloss

Trim Color _____
- ☐ Flat ☐ Satin
- ☐ Matte ☐ Semi gloss
- ☐ Eggshell ☐ High gloss

Notes

Date _____

Job Name _____

ph # _____

Job Address _____

Paint Brand _____

Room Name _____

Wall Color _____

☐ Flat	☐ Satin
☐ Matte	☐ Semi gloss
☐ Eggshell	☐ High gloss

Ceiling Color _____

☐ Flat	☐ Satin
☐ Matte	☐ Semi gloss
☐ Eggshell	☐ High gloss

Trim Color _____

☐ Flat	☐ Satin
☐ Matte	☐ Semi gloss
☐ Eggshell	☐ High gloss

Notes

Room Name _____

Wall Color _____

☐ Flat	☐ Satin
☐ Matte	☐ Semi gloss
☐ Eggshell	☐ High gloss

Ceiling Color _____

☐ Flat	☐ Satin
☐ Matte	☐ Semi gloss
☐ Eggshell	☐ High gloss

Trim Color _____

☐ Flat	☐ Satin
☐ Matte	☐ Semi gloss
☐ Eggshell	☐ High gloss

Notes

Date _____

Job Name _____ ph # _____

Job Address _____

Paint Brand _____

Room Name _____

Wall Color _____
- ☐ Flat ☐ Satin
- ☐ Matte ☐ Semi gloss
- ☐ Eggshell ☐ High gloss

Ceiling Color _____
- ☐ Flat ☐ Satin
- ☐ Matte ☐ Semi gloss
- ☐ Eggshell ☐ High gloss

Trim Color _____
- ☐ Flat ☐ Satin
- ☐ Matte ☐ Semi gloss
- ☐ Eggshell ☐ High gloss

Notes

Room Name _____

Wall Color _____
- ☐ Flat ☐ Satin
- ☐ Matte ☐ Semi gloss
- ☐ Eggshell ☐ High gloss

Ceiling Color _____
- ☐ Flat ☐ Satin
- ☐ Matte ☐ Semi gloss
- ☐ Eggshell ☐ High gloss

Trim Color _____
- ☐ Flat ☐ Satin
- ☐ Matte ☐ Semi gloss
- ☐ Eggshell ☐ High gloss

Notes

Date _____

Job Name _____ ph # _____

Job Address _____

Paint Brand _____

Room Name _____

Wall Color _____

- [ ] Flat
- [ ] Matte
- [ ] Eggshell
- [ ] Satin
- [ ] Semi gloss
- [ ] High gloss

Ceiling Color _____

- [ ] Flat
- [ ] Matte
- [ ] Eggshell
- [ ] Satin
- [ ] Semi gloss
- [ ] High gloss

Trim Color _____

- [ ] Flat
- [ ] Matte
- [ ] Eggshell
- [ ] Satin
- [ ] Semi gloss
- [ ] High gloss

Notes

Room Name _____

Wall Color _____

- [ ] Flat
- [ ] Matte
- [ ] Eggshell
- [ ] Satin
- [ ] Semi gloss
- [ ] High gloss

Ceiling Color _____

- [ ] Flat
- [ ] Matte
- [ ] Eggshell
- [ ] Satin
- [ ] Semi gloss
- [ ] High gloss

Trim Color _____

- [ ] Flat
- [ ] Matte
- [ ] Eggshell
- [ ] Satin
- [ ] Semi gloss
- [ ] High gloss

Notes

Date _____

Job Name _____   ph # _____

Job Address _____

Paint Brand _____

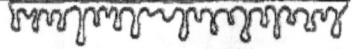

Room Name _____

Wall Color _____

☐ Flat	☐ Satin
☐ Matte	☐ Semi gloss
☐ Eggshell	☐ High gloss

Ceiling Color _____

☐ Flat	☐ Satin
☐ Matte	☐ Semi gloss
☐ Eggshell	☐ High gloss

Trim Color _____

☐ Flat	☐ Satin
☐ Matte	☐ Semi gloss
☐ Eggshell	☐ High gloss

Notes

Room Name _____

Wall Color _____

☐ Flat	☐ Satin
☐ Matte	☐ Semi gloss
☐ Eggshell	☐ High gloss

Ceiling Color _____

☐ Flat	☐ Satin
☐ Matte	☐ Semi gloss
☐ Eggshell	☐ High gloss

Trim Color _____

☐ Flat	☐ Satin
☐ Matte	☐ Semi gloss
☐ Eggshell	☐ High gloss

Notes

Date _____

Job Name _____ ph # _____

Job Address _____

Paint Brand _____

Room Name
_____

Wall Color _____
- ☐ Flat ☐ Satin
- ☐ Matte ☐ Semi gloss
- ☐ Eggshell ☐ High gloss

Ceiling Color _____
- ☐ Flat ☐ Satin
- ☐ Matte ☐ Semi gloss
- ☐ Eggshell ☐ High gloss

Trim Color _____
- ☐ Flat ☐ Satin
- ☐ Matte ☐ Semi gloss
- ☐ Eggshell ☐ High gloss

Notes

Room Name
_____

Wall Color _____
- ☐ Flat ☐ Satin
- ☐ Matte ☐ Semi gloss
- ☐ Eggshell ☐ High gloss

Ceiling Color _____
- ☐ Flat ☐ Satin
- ☐ Matte ☐ Semi gloss
- ☐ Eggshell ☐ High gloss

Trim Color _____
- ☐ Flat ☐ Satin
- ☐ Matte ☐ Semi gloss
- ☐ Eggshell ☐ High gloss

Notes

Date

Job Name   ph #

Job Address

Paint Brand

Room Name

Wall Color
- ☐ Flat ☐ Satin
- ☐ Matte ☐ Semi gloss
- ☐ Eggshell ☐ High gloss

Ceiling Color
- ☐ Flat ☐ Satin
- ☐ Matte ☐ Semi gloss
- ☐ Eggshell ☐ High gloss

Trim Color
- ☐ Flat ☐ Satin
- ☐ Matte ☐ Semi gloss
- ☐ Eggshell ☐ High gloss

Notes

Room Name

Wall Color
- ☐ Flat ☐ Satin
- ☐ Matte ☐ Semi gloss
- ☐ Eggshell ☐ High gloss

Ceiling Color
- ☐ Flat ☐ Satin
- ☐ Matte ☐ Semi gloss
- ☐ Eggshell ☐ High gloss

Trim Color
- ☐ Flat ☐ Satin
- ☐ Matte ☐ Semi gloss
- ☐ Eggshell ☐ High gloss

Notes

Date _____

Job Name _____ ph # _____

Job Address _____

Paint Brand _____

Room Name _____

Wall Color _____
- ☐ Flat ☐ Satin
- ☐ Matte ☐ Semi gloss
- ☐ Eggshell ☐ High gloss

Ceiling Color _____
- ☐ Flat ☐ Satin
- ☐ Matte ☐ Semi gloss
- ☐ Eggshell ☐ High gloss

Trim Color _____
- ☐ Flat ☐ Satin
- ☐ Matte ☐ Semi gloss
- ☐ Eggshell ☐ High gloss

Notes

Room Name _____

Wall Color _____
- ☐ Flat ☐ Satin
- ☐ Matte ☐ Semi gloss
- ☐ Eggshell ☐ High gloss

Ceiling Color _____
- ☐ Flat ☐ Satin
- ☐ Matte ☐ Semi gloss
- ☐ Eggshell ☐ High gloss

Trim Color _____
- ☐ Flat ☐ Satin
- ☐ Matte ☐ Semi gloss
- ☐ Eggshell ☐ High gloss

Notes

Date _____

Job Name _____ ph # _____

Job Address _____

Paint Brand _____

Room Name

Wall Color _____

- [ ] Flat
- [ ] Matte
- [ ] Eggshell
- [ ] Satin
- [ ] Semi gloss
- [ ] High gloss

Ceiling Color _____

- [ ] Flat
- [ ] Matte
- [ ] Eggshell
- [ ] Satin
- [ ] Semi gloss
- [ ] High gloss

Trim Color _____

- [ ] Flat
- [ ] Matte
- [ ] Eggshell
- [ ] Satin
- [ ] Semi gloss
- [ ] High gloss

Notes

Room Name

Wall Color _____

- [ ] Flat
- [ ] Matte
- [ ] Eggshell
- [ ] Satin
- [ ] Semi gloss
- [ ] High gloss

Ceiling Color _____

- [ ] Flat
- [ ] Matte
- [ ] Eggshell
- [ ] Satin
- [ ] Semi gloss
- [ ] High gloss

Trim Color _____

- [ ] Flat
- [ ] Matte
- [ ] Eggshell
- [ ] Satin
- [ ] Semi gloss
- [ ] High gloss

Notes

Date _____

Job Name _____ ph # _____

Job Address _____

Paint Brand _____

Room Name _____

Wall Color _____

☐ Flat   ☐ Satin
☐ Matte   ☐ Semi gloss
☐ Eggshell ☐ High gloss

Ceiling Color _____

☐ Flat   ☐ Satin
☐ Matte   ☐ Semi gloss
☐ Eggshell ☐ High gloss

Trim Color _____

☐ Flat   ☐ Satin
☐ Matte   ☐ Semi gloss
☐ Eggshell ☐ High gloss

Notes

Room Name _____

Wall Color _____

☐ Flat   ☐ Satin
☐ Matte   ☐ Semi gloss
☐ Eggshell ☐ High gloss

Ceiling Color _____

☐ Flat   ☐ Satin
☐ Matte   ☐ Semi gloss
☐ Eggshell ☐ High gloss

Trim Color _____

☐ Flat   ☐ Satin
☐ Matte   ☐ Semi gloss
☐ Eggshell ☐ High gloss

Notes

Date _____

Job Name _____ ph # _____

Job Address _____

Paint Brand _____

Room Name _____

Wall Color _____	☐ Flat ☐ Satin ☐ Matte ☐ Semi gloss ☐ Eggshell ☐ High gloss
Ceiling Color _____	☐ Flat ☐ Satin ☐ Matte ☐ Semi gloss ☐ Eggshell ☐ High gloss
Trim Color _____	☐ Flat ☐ Satin ☐ Matte ☐ Semi gloss ☐ Eggshell ☐ High gloss

Notes

Room Name _____

Wall Color _____	☐ Flat ☐ Satin ☐ Matte ☐ Semi gloss ☐ Eggshell ☐ High gloss
Ceiling Color _____	☐ Flat ☐ Satin ☐ Matte ☐ Semi gloss ☐ Eggshell ☐ High gloss
Trim Color _____	☐ Flat ☐ Satin ☐ Matte ☐ Semi gloss ☐ Eggshell ☐ High gloss

Notes

Date _____

Job Name _____ ph # _____

Job Address _____

Paint Brand _____

Room Name
_____

Wall Color _____
☐ Flat   ☐ Satin
☐ Matte   ☐ Semi gloss
☐ Eggshell ☐ High gloss

Ceiling Color _____
☐ Flat   ☐ Satin
☐ Matte   ☐ Semi gloss
☐ Eggshell ☐ High gloss

Trim Color _____
☐ Flat   ☐ Satin
☐ Matte   ☐ Semi gloss
☐ Eggshell ☐ High gloss

Notes

Room Name
_____

Wall Color _____
☐ Flat   ☐ Satin
☐ Matte   ☐ Semi gloss
☐ Eggshell ☐ High gloss

Ceiling Color _____
☐ Flat   ☐ Satin
☐ Matte   ☐ Semi gloss
☐ Eggshell ☐ High gloss

Trim Color _____
☐ Flat   ☐ Satin
☐ Matte   ☐ Semi gloss
☐ Eggshell ☐ High gloss

Notes

Date _____

Job Name _____ ph # _____

Job Address _____

Paint Brand _____

Room Name _____

Wall Color _____
- ☐ Flat ☐ Satin
- ☐ Matte ☐ Semi gloss
- ☐ Eggshell ☐ High gloss

Ceiling Color _____
- ☐ Flat ☐ Satin
- ☐ Matte ☐ Semi gloss
- ☐ Eggshell ☐ High gloss

Trim Color _____
- ☐ Flat ☐ Satin
- ☐ Matte ☐ Semi gloss
- ☐ Eggshell ☐ High gloss

Notes

Room Name _____

Wall Color _____
- ☐ Flat ☐ Satin
- ☐ Matte ☐ Semi gloss
- ☐ Eggshell ☐ High gloss

Ceiling Color _____
- ☐ Flat ☐ Satin
- ☐ Matte ☐ Semi gloss
- ☐ Eggshell ☐ High gloss

Trim Color _____
- ☐ Flat ☐ Satin
- ☐ Matte ☐ Semi gloss
- ☐ Eggshell ☐ High gloss

Notes

Date _____

Job Name _____   ph # _____

Job Address _____

Paint Brand _____

Room Name
_____

☐ Flat	☐ Satin
☐ Matte	☐ Semi gloss
☐ Eggshell	☐ High gloss

Wall Color _____

☐ Flat	☐ Satin
☐ Matte	☐ Semi gloss
☐ Eggshell	☐ High gloss

Ceiling Color _____

☐ Flat	☐ Satin
☐ Matte	☐ Semi gloss
☐ Eggshell	☐ High gloss

Trim Color _____

Notes

Room Name
_____

☐ Flat	☐ Satin
☐ Matte	☐ Semi gloss
☐ Eggshell	☐ High gloss

Wall Color _____

☐ Flat	☐ Satin
☐ Matte	☐ Semi gloss
☐ Eggshell	☐ High gloss

Ceiling Color _____

☐ Flat	☐ Satin
☐ Matte	☐ Semi gloss
☐ Eggshell	☐ High gloss

Trim Color _____

Notes

Date _____

Job Name _____ ph # _____

Job Address _____

Paint Brand _____

Room Name _____

Wall Color _____

- ☐ Flat ☐ Satin
- ☐ Matte ☐ Semi gloss
- ☐ Eggshell ☐ High gloss

Ceiling Color _____

- ☐ Flat ☐ Satin
- ☐ Matte ☐ Semi gloss
- ☐ Eggshell ☐ High gloss

Trim Color _____

- ☐ Flat ☐ Satin
- ☐ Matte ☐ Semi gloss
- ☐ Eggshell ☐ High gloss

Notes

Room Name _____

Wall Color _____

- ☐ Flat ☐ Satin
- ☐ Matte ☐ Semi gloss
- ☐ Eggshell ☐ High gloss

Ceiling Color _____

- ☐ Flat ☐ Satin
- ☐ Matte ☐ Semi gloss
- ☐ Eggshell ☐ High gloss

Trim Color _____

- ☐ Flat ☐ Satin
- ☐ Matte ☐ Semi gloss
- ☐ Eggshell ☐ High gloss

Notes

Date _____

Job Name _____ ph # _____

Job Address _____

Paint Brand _____

Room Name

	Flat	Satin
	Matte	Semi gloss
Wall Color	Eggshell	High gloss
	Flat	Satin
	Matte	Semi gloss
Ceiling Color	Eggshell	High gloss
	Flat	Satin
	Matte	Semi gloss
Trim Color	Eggshell	High gloss

Notes

Room Name

	Flat	Satin
	Matte	Semi gloss
Wall Color	Eggshell	High gloss
	Flat	Satin
	Matte	Semi gloss
Ceiling Color	Eggshell	High gloss
	Flat	Satin
	Matte	Semi gloss
Trim Color	Eggshell	High gloss

Notes

Date _____

Job Name _____ ph # _____

Job Address _____

Paint Brand _____

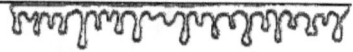

Room Name _____

Wall Color _____
- ☐ Flat   ☐ Satin
- ☐ Matte   ☐ Semi gloss
- ☐ Eggshell   ☐ High gloss

Ceiling Color _____
- ☐ Flat   ☐ Satin
- ☐ Matte   ☐ Semi gloss
- ☐ Eggshell   ☐ High gloss

Trim Color _____
- ☐ Flat   ☐ Satin
- ☐ Matte   ☐ Semi gloss
- ☐ Eggshell   ☐ High gloss

Notes

Room Name _____

Wall Color _____
- ☐ Flat   ☐ Satin
- ☐ Matte   ☐ Semi gloss
- ☐ Eggshell   ☐ High gloss

Ceiling Color _____
- ☐ Flat   ☐ Satin
- ☐ Matte   ☐ Semi gloss
- ☐ Eggshell   ☐ High gloss

Trim Color _____
- ☐ Flat   ☐ Satin
- ☐ Matte   ☐ Semi gloss
- ☐ Eggshell   ☐ High gloss

Notes

Date _____

Job Name _____ ph # _____

Job Address _____

Paint Brand _____

Room Name
_____

Wall Color _____
☐ Flat ☐ Satin
☐ Matte ☐ Semi gloss
☐ Eggshell ☐ High gloss

Ceiling Color _____
☐ Flat ☐ Satin
☐ Matte ☐ Semi gloss
☐ Eggshell ☐ High gloss

Trim Color _____
☐ Flat ☐ Satin
☐ Matte ☐ Semi gloss
☐ Eggshell ☐ High gloss

Notes

Room Name
_____

Wall Color _____
☐ Flat ☐ Satin
☐ Matte ☐ Semi gloss
☐ Eggshell ☐ High gloss

Ceiling Color _____
☐ Flat ☐ Satin
☐ Matte ☐ Semi gloss
☐ Eggshell ☐ High gloss

Trim Color _____
☐ Flat ☐ Satin
☐ Matte ☐ Semi gloss
☐ Eggshell ☐ High gloss

Notes

Date

Job Name   ph #

Job Address

Paint Brand

Room Name

Wall Color
- ☐ Flat ☐ Satin
- ☐ Matte ☐ Semi gloss
- ☐ Eggshell ☐ High gloss

Ceiling Color
- ☐ Flat ☐ Satin
- ☐ Matte ☐ Semi gloss
- ☐ Eggshell ☐ High gloss

Trim Color
- ☐ Flat ☐ Satin
- ☐ Matte ☐ Semi gloss
- ☐ Eggshell ☐ High gloss

Notes

Room Name

Wall Color
- ☐ Flat ☐ Satin
- ☐ Matte ☐ Semi gloss
- ☐ Eggshell ☐ High gloss

Ceiling Color
- ☐ Flat ☐ Satin
- ☐ Matte ☐ Semi gloss
- ☐ Eggshell ☐ High gloss

Trim Color
- ☐ Flat ☐ Satin
- ☐ Matte ☐ Semi gloss
- ☐ Eggshell ☐ High gloss

Notes

Date _____

Job Name _____ ph # _____

Job Address _____

Paint Brand _____

Room Name
_____

Wall Color _____

☐ Flat	☐ Satin
☐ Matte	☐ Semi gloss
☐ Eggshell	☐ High gloss

Ceiling Color _____

☐ Flat	☐ Satin
☐ Matte	☐ Semi gloss
☐ Eggshell	☐ High gloss

Trim Color _____

☐ Flat	☐ Satin
☐ Matte	☐ Semi gloss
☐ Eggshell	☐ High gloss

Notes

Room Name
_____

Wall Color _____

☐ Flat	☐ Satin
☐ Matte	☐ Semi gloss
☐ Eggshell	☐ High gloss

Ceiling Color _____

☐ Flat	☐ Satin
☐ Matte	☐ Semi gloss
☐ Eggshell	☐ High gloss

Trim Color _____

☐ Flat	☐ Satin
☐ Matte	☐ Semi gloss
☐ Eggshell	☐ High gloss

Notes

Date _____

Job Name _____ ph # _____

Job Address _____

Paint Brand _____

Room Name _____

Wall Color _____
- ☐ Flat
- ☐ Matte
- ☐ Eggshell
- ☐ Satin
- ☐ Semi gloss
- ☐ High gloss

Ceiling Color _____
- ☐ Flat
- ☐ Matte
- ☐ Eggshell
- ☐ Satin
- ☐ Semi gloss
- ☐ High gloss

Trim Color _____
- ☐ Flat
- ☐ Matte
- ☐ Eggshell
- ☐ Satin
- ☐ Semi gloss
- ☐ High gloss

Notes

Room Name _____

Wall Color _____
- ☐ Flat
- ☐ Matte
- ☐ Eggshell
- ☐ Satin
- ☐ Semi gloss
- ☐ High gloss

Ceiling Color _____
- ☐ Flat
- ☐ Matte
- ☐ Eggshell
- ☐ Satin
- ☐ Semi gloss
- ☐ High gloss

Trim Color _____
- ☐ Flat
- ☐ Matte
- ☐ Eggshell
- ☐ Satin
- ☐ Semi gloss
- ☐ High gloss

Notes

Date _____

Job Name _____ ph # _____

Job Address _____

Paint Brand _____

Room Name _____

Wall Color _____

- ☐ Flat   ☐ Satin
- ☐ Matte   ☐ Semi gloss
- ☐ Eggshell   ☐ High gloss

Ceiling Color _____

- ☐ Flat   ☐ Satin
- ☐ Matte   ☐ Semi gloss
- ☐ Eggshell   ☐ High gloss

Trim Color _____

- ☐ Flat   ☐ Satin
- ☐ Matte   ☐ Semi gloss
- ☐ Eggshell   ☐ High gloss

Notes

Room Name _____

Wall Color _____

- ☐ Flat   ☐ Satin
- ☐ Matte   ☐ Semi gloss
- ☐ Eggshell   ☐ High gloss

Ceiling Color _____

- ☐ Flat   ☐ Satin
- ☐ Matte   ☐ Semi gloss
- ☐ Eggshell   ☐ High gloss

Trim Color _____

- ☐ Flat   ☐ Satin
- ☐ Matte   ☐ Semi gloss
- ☐ Eggshell   ☐ High gloss

Notes

Date _____

Job Name _____   ph # _____

Job Address _____

Paint Brand _____

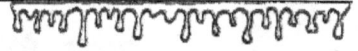

Room Name _____

Wall Color _____
- ☐ Flat   ☐ Satin
- ☐ Matte   ☐ Semi gloss
- ☐ Eggshell   ☐ High gloss

Ceiling Color _____
- ☐ Flat   ☐ Satin
- ☐ Matte   ☐ Semi gloss
- ☐ Eggshell   ☐ High gloss

Trim Color _____
- ☐ Flat   ☐ Satin
- ☐ Matte   ☐ Semi gloss
- ☐ Eggshell   ☐ High gloss

Notes

Room Name _____

Wall Color _____
- ☐ Flat   ☐ Satin
- ☐ Matte   ☐ Semi gloss
- ☐ Eggshell   ☐ High gloss

Ceiling Color _____
- ☐ Flat   ☐ Satin
- ☐ Matte   ☐ Semi gloss
- ☐ Eggshell   ☐ High gloss

Trim Color _____
- ☐ Flat   ☐ Satin
- ☐ Matte   ☐ Semi gloss
- ☐ Eggshell   ☐ High gloss

Notes

Date _____

Job Name _____ ph # _____

Job Address _____

Paint Brand _____

Room Name
_____

Wall Color _____
☐ Flat ☐ Satin
☐ Matte ☐ Semi gloss
☐ Eggshell ☐ High gloss

Ceiling Color _____
☐ Flat ☐ Satin
☐ Matte ☐ Semi gloss
☐ Eggshell ☐ High gloss

Trim Color _____
☐ Flat ☐ Satin
☐ Matte ☐ Semi gloss
☐ Eggshell ☐ High gloss

Notes

Room Name
_____

Wall Color _____
☐ Flat ☐ Satin
☐ Matte ☐ Semi gloss
☐ Eggshell ☐ High gloss

Ceiling Color _____
☐ Flat ☐ Satin
☐ Matte ☐ Semi gloss
☐ Eggshell ☐ High gloss

Trim Color _____
☐ Flat ☐ Satin
☐ Matte ☐ Semi gloss
☐ Eggshell ☐ High gloss

Notes

Date

Job Name   ph #

Job Address

Paint Brand

Room Name

Wall Color
☐ Flat   ☐ Satin
☐ Matte   ☐ Semi gloss
☐ Eggshell ☐ High gloss

Ceiling Color
☐ Flat   ☐ Satin
☐ Matte   ☐ Semi gloss
☐ Eggshell ☐ High gloss

Trim Color
☐ Flat   ☐ Satin
☐ Matte   ☐ Semi gloss
☐ Eggshell ☐ High gloss

Notes

Room Name

Wall Color
☐ Flat   ☐ Satin
☐ Matte   ☐ Semi gloss
☐ Eggshell ☐ High gloss

Ceiling Color
☐ Flat   ☐ Satin
☐ Matte   ☐ Semi gloss
☐ Eggshell ☐ High gloss

Trim Color
☐ Flat   ☐ Satin
☐ Matte   ☐ Semi gloss
☐ Eggshell ☐ High gloss

Notes

Date _____

Job Name _____ ph # _____

Job Address _____

Paint Brand _____

Room Name _____

Wall Color _____

☐ Flat	☐ Satin		
☐ Matte	☐ Semi gloss		
☐ Eggshell	☐ High gloss		

Ceiling Color _____

☐ Flat	☐ Satin		
☐ Matte	☐ Semi gloss		
☐ Eggshell	☐ High gloss		

Trim Color _____

☐ Flat	☐ Satin		
☐ Matte	☐ Semi gloss		
☐ Eggshell	☐ High gloss		

Notes

Room Name _____

Wall Color _____

☐ Flat	☐ Satin		
☐ Matte	☐ Semi gloss		
☐ Eggshell	☐ High gloss		

Ceiling Color _____

☐ Flat	☐ Satin		
☐ Matte	☐ Semi gloss		
☐ Eggshell	☐ High gloss		

Trim Color _____

☐ Flat	☐ Satin		
☐ Matte	☐ Semi gloss		
☐ Eggshell	☐ High gloss		

Notes

Date _____

Job Name _____ ph # _____

Job Address _____

Paint Brand _____

Room Name _____

Wall Color _____
- ☐ Flat ☐ Satin
- ☐ Matte ☐ Semi gloss
- ☐ Eggshell ☐ High gloss

Ceiling Color _____
- ☐ Flat ☐ Satin
- ☐ Matte ☐ Semi gloss
- ☐ Eggshell ☐ High gloss

Trim Color _____
- ☐ Flat ☐ Satin
- ☐ Matte ☐ Semi gloss
- ☐ Eggshell ☐ High gloss

Notes

Room Name _____

Wall Color _____
- ☐ Flat ☐ Satin
- ☐ Matte ☐ Semi gloss
- ☐ Eggshell ☐ High gloss

Ceiling Color _____
- ☐ Flat ☐ Satin
- ☐ Matte ☐ Semi gloss
- ☐ Eggshell ☐ High gloss

Trim Color _____
- ☐ Flat ☐ Satin
- ☐ Matte ☐ Semi gloss
- ☐ Eggshell ☐ High gloss

Notes

Date _____

Job Name _____ ph # _____

Job Address _____

Paint Brand _____

Room Name
_____

Wall Color _____
- ☐ Flat ☐ Satin
- ☐ Matte ☐ Semi gloss
- ☐ Eggshell ☐ High gloss

Ceiling Color _____
- ☐ Flat ☐ Satin
- ☐ Matte ☐ Semi gloss
- ☐ Eggshell ☐ High gloss

Trim Color _____
- ☐ Flat ☐ Satin
- ☐ Matte ☐ Semi gloss
- ☐ Eggshell ☐ High gloss

Notes

Room Name
_____

Wall Color _____
- ☐ Flat ☐ Satin
- ☐ Matte ☐ Semi gloss
- ☐ Eggshell ☐ High gloss

Ceiling Color _____
- ☐ Flat ☐ Satin
- ☐ Matte ☐ Semi gloss
- ☐ Eggshell ☐ High gloss

Trim Color _____
- ☐ Flat ☐ Satin
- ☐ Matte ☐ Semi gloss
- ☐ Eggshell ☐ High gloss

Notes

Date _____

Job Name _____ ph # _____

Job Address _____

Paint Brand _____

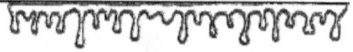

Room Name _____

Wall Color	☐ Flat ☐ Matte ☐ Eggshell	☐ Satin ☐ Semi gloss ☐ High gloss
Ceiling Color	☐ Flat ☐ Matte ☐ Eggshell	☐ Satin ☐ Semi gloss ☐ High gloss
Trim Color	☐ Flat ☐ Matte ☐ Eggshell	☐ Satin ☐ Semi gloss ☐ High gloss

Notes

Room Name _____

Wall Color	☐ Flat ☐ Matte ☐ Eggshell	☐ Satin ☐ Semi gloss ☐ High gloss
Ceiling Color	☐ Flat ☐ Matte ☐ Eggshell	☐ Satin ☐ Semi gloss ☐ High gloss
Trim Color	☐ Flat ☐ Matte ☐ Eggshell	☐ Satin ☐ Semi gloss ☐ High gloss

Notes

Date _____

Job Name _____ ph # _____

Job Address _____

Paint Brand _____

Room Name _____

Wall Color _____
☐ Flat   ☐ Satin
☐ Matte   ☐ Semi gloss
☐ Eggshell   ☐ High gloss

Ceiling Color _____
☐ Flat   ☐ Satin
☐ Matte   ☐ Semi gloss
☐ Eggshell   ☐ High gloss

Trim Color _____
☐ Flat   ☐ Satin
☐ Matte   ☐ Semi gloss
☐ Eggshell   ☐ High gloss

Notes

Room Name _____

Wall Color _____
☐ Flat   ☐ Satin
☐ Matte   ☐ Semi gloss
☐ Eggshell   ☐ High gloss

Ceiling Color _____
☐ Flat   ☐ Satin
☐ Matte   ☐ Semi gloss
☐ Eggshell   ☐ High gloss

Trim Color _____
☐ Flat   ☐ Satin
☐ Matte   ☐ Semi gloss
☐ Eggshell   ☐ High gloss

Notes

Date _____

Job Name _____ ph # _____

Job Address _____

Paint Brand _____

Room Name

Wall Color _____

☐ Flat ☐ Satin
☐ Matte ☐ Semi gloss
☐ Eggshell ☐ High gloss

Ceiling Color _____

☐ Flat ☐ Satin
☐ Matte ☐ Semi gloss
☐ Eggshell ☐ High gloss

Trim Color _____

☐ Flat ☐ Satin
☐ Matte ☐ Semi gloss
☐ Eggshell ☐ High gloss

Notes

Room Name

Wall Color _____

☐ Flat ☐ Satin
☐ Matte ☐ Semi gloss
☐ Eggshell ☐ High gloss

Ceiling Color _____

☐ Flat ☐ Satin
☐ Matte ☐ Semi gloss
☐ Eggshell ☐ High gloss

Trim Color _____

☐ Flat ☐ Satin
☐ Matte ☐ Semi gloss
☐ Eggshell ☐ High gloss

Notes

Date _____

Job Name _____   ph # _____

Job Address _____

Paint Brand _____

Room Name

Wall Color _____
- ☐ Flat   ☐ Satin
- ☐ Matte   ☐ Semi gloss
- ☐ Eggshell ☐ High gloss

Ceiling Color _____
- ☐ Flat   ☐ Satin
- ☐ Matte   ☐ Semi gloss
- ☐ Eggshell ☐ High gloss

Trim Color _____
- ☐ Flat   ☐ Satin
- ☐ Matte   ☐ Semi gloss
- ☐ Eggshell ☐ High gloss

Notes

Room Name

Wall Color _____
- ☐ Flat   ☐ Satin
- ☐ Matte   ☐ Semi gloss
- ☐ Eggshell ☐ High gloss

Ceiling Color _____
- ☐ Flat   ☐ Satin
- ☐ Matte   ☐ Semi gloss
- ☐ Eggshell ☐ High gloss

Trim Color _____
- ☐ Flat   ☐ Satin
- ☐ Matte   ☐ Semi gloss
- ☐ Eggshell ☐ High gloss

Notes

Date _____

Job Name _____ ph # _____

Job Address _____

Paint Brand _____

Room Name _____

Wall Color	☐ Flat	☐ Satin
	☐ Matte	☐ Semi gloss
	☐ Eggshell	☐ High gloss
Ceiling Color	☐ Flat	☐ Satin
	☐ Matte	☐ Semi gloss
	☐ Eggshell	☐ High gloss
Trim Color	☐ Flat	☐ Satin
	☐ Matte	☐ Semi gloss
	☐ Eggshell	☐ High gloss

Notes

Room Name _____

Wall Color	☐ Flat	☐ Satin
	☐ Matte	☐ Semi gloss
	☐ Eggshell	☐ High gloss
Ceiling Color	☐ Flat	☐ Satin
	☐ Matte	☐ Semi gloss
	☐ Eggshell	☐ High gloss
Trim Color	☐ Flat	☐ Satin
	☐ Matte	☐ Semi gloss
	☐ Eggshell	☐ High gloss

Notes

Date _____

Job Name _____ ph # _____

Job Address _____

Paint Brand _____

Room Name
_____

Wall Color _____
☐ Flat ☐ Satin
☐ Matte ☐ Semi gloss
☐ Eggshell ☐ High gloss

Ceiling Color _____
☐ Flat ☐ Satin
☐ Matte ☐ Semi gloss
☐ Eggshell ☐ High gloss

Trim Color _____
☐ Flat ☐ Satin
☐ Matte ☐ Semi gloss
☐ Eggshell ☐ High gloss

Notes

Room Name
_____

Wall Color _____
☐ Flat ☐ Satin
☐ Matte ☐ Semi gloss
☐ Eggshell ☐ High gloss

Ceiling Color _____
☐ Flat ☐ Satin
☐ Matte ☐ Semi gloss
☐ Eggshell ☐ High gloss

Trim Color _____
☐ Flat ☐ Satin
☐ Matte ☐ Semi gloss
☐ Eggshell ☐ High gloss

Notes

Date _____

Job Name _____ ph # _____

Job Address _____

Paint Brand _____

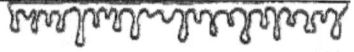

Room Name _____

Wall Color _____
☐ Flat   ☐ Satin
☐ Matte ☐ Semi gloss
☐ Eggshell ☐ High gloss

Ceiling Color _____
☐ Flat   ☐ Satin
☐ Matte ☐ Semi gloss
☐ Eggshell ☐ High gloss

Trim Color _____
☐ Flat   ☐ Satin
☐ Matte ☐ Semi gloss
☐ Eggshell ☐ High gloss

Notes

Room Name _____

Wall Color _____
☐ Flat   ☐ Satin
☐ Matte ☐ Semi gloss
☐ Eggshell ☐ High gloss

Ceiling Color _____
☐ Flat   ☐ Satin
☐ Matte ☐ Semi gloss
☐ Eggshell ☐ High gloss

Trim Color _____
☐ Flat   ☐ Satin
☐ Matte ☐ Semi gloss
☐ Eggshell ☐ High gloss

Notes

Date _____

Job Name _____ ph # _____

Job Address _____

Paint Brand _____

Room Name _____

Wall Color _____
- ☐ Flat ☐ Satin
- ☐ Matte ☐ Semi gloss
- ☐ Eggshell ☐ High gloss

Ceiling Color _____
- ☐ Flat ☐ Satin
- ☐ Matte ☐ Semi gloss
- ☐ Eggshell ☐ High gloss

Trim Color _____
- ☐ Flat ☐ Satin
- ☐ Matte ☐ Semi gloss
- ☐ Eggshell ☐ High gloss

Notes

Room Name _____

Wall Color _____
- ☐ Flat ☐ Satin
- ☐ Matte ☐ Semi gloss
- ☐ Eggshell ☐ High gloss

Ceiling Color _____
- ☐ Flat ☐ Satin
- ☐ Matte ☐ Semi gloss
- ☐ Eggshell ☐ High gloss

Trim Color _____
- ☐ Flat ☐ Satin
- ☐ Matte ☐ Semi gloss
- ☐ Eggshell ☐ High gloss

Notes

Date _____

Job Name _____ ph # _____

Job Address _____

Paint Brand _____

Room Name _____

Wall Color _____
- ☐ Flat ☐ Satin
- ☐ Matte ☐ Semi gloss
- ☐ Eggshell ☐ High gloss

Ceiling Color _____
- ☐ Flat ☐ Satin
- ☐ Matte ☐ Semi gloss
- ☐ Eggshell ☐ High gloss

Trim Color _____
- ☐ Flat ☐ Satin
- ☐ Matte ☐ Semi gloss
- ☐ Eggshell ☐ High gloss

Notes

Room Name _____

Wall Color _____
- ☐ Flat ☐ Satin
- ☐ Matte ☐ Semi gloss
- ☐ Eggshell ☐ High gloss

Ceiling Color _____
- ☐ Flat ☐ Satin
- ☐ Matte ☐ Semi gloss
- ☐ Eggshell ☐ High gloss

Trim Color _____
- ☐ Flat ☐ Satin
- ☐ Matte ☐ Semi gloss
- ☐ Eggshell ☐ High gloss

Notes

Date _____

Job Name _____ ph # _____

Job Address _____

Paint Brand _____

Room Name

Wall Color _____
- ☐ Flat   ☐ Satin
- ☐ Matte   ☐ Semi gloss
- ☐ Eggshell ☐ High gloss

Ceiling Color _____
- ☐ Flat   ☐ Satin
- ☐ Matte   ☐ Semi gloss
- ☐ Eggshell ☐ High gloss

Trim Color _____
- ☐ Flat   ☐ Satin
- ☐ Matte   ☐ Semi gloss
- ☐ Eggshell ☐ High gloss

Notes

Room Name

Wall Color _____
- ☐ Flat   ☐ Satin
- ☐ Matte   ☐ Semi gloss
- ☐ Eggshell ☐ High gloss

Ceiling Color _____
- ☐ Flat   ☐ Satin
- ☐ Matte   ☐ Semi gloss
- ☐ Eggshell ☐ High gloss

Trim Color _____
- ☐ Flat   ☐ Satin
- ☐ Matte   ☐ Semi gloss
- ☐ Eggshell ☐ High gloss

Notes

Date _____

Job Name _____ ph # _____

Job Address _____

Paint Brand _____

Room Name

Wall Color _____
- [ ] Flat [ ] Satin
- [ ] Matte [ ] Semi gloss
- [ ] Eggshell [ ] High gloss

Ceiling Color _____
- [ ] Flat [ ] Satin
- [ ] Matte [ ] Semi gloss
- [ ] Eggshell [ ] High gloss

Trim Color _____
- [ ] Flat [ ] Satin
- [ ] Matte [ ] Semi gloss
- [ ] Eggshell [ ] High gloss

Notes

Room Name

Wall Color _____
- [ ] Flat [ ] Satin
- [ ] Matte [ ] Semi gloss
- [ ] Eggshell [ ] High gloss

Ceiling Color _____
- [ ] Flat [ ] Satin
- [ ] Matte [ ] Semi gloss
- [ ] Eggshell [ ] High gloss

Trim Color _____
- [ ] Flat [ ] Satin
- [ ] Matte [ ] Semi gloss
- [ ] Eggshell [ ] High gloss

Notes

Date _____

Job Name _____ ph # _____

Job Address _____

Paint Brand _____

Room Name

Wall Color _____

☐ Flat ☐ Satin
☐ Matte ☐ Semi gloss
☐ Eggshell ☐ High gloss

Ceiling Color _____

☐ Flat ☐ Satin
☐ Matte ☐ Semi gloss
☐ Eggshell ☐ High gloss

Trim Color _____

☐ Flat ☐ Satin
☐ Matte ☐ Semi gloss
☐ Eggshell ☐ High gloss

Notes

Room Name

Wall Color _____

☐ Flat ☐ Satin
☐ Matte ☐ Semi gloss
☐ Eggshell ☐ High gloss

Ceiling Color _____

☐ Flat ☐ Satin
☐ Matte ☐ Semi gloss
☐ Eggshell ☐ High gloss

Trim Color _____

☐ Flat ☐ Satin
☐ Matte ☐ Semi gloss
☐ Eggshell ☐ High gloss

Notes

Date _____

Job Name _____ ph # _____

Job Address _____

Paint Brand _____

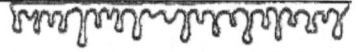

Room Name _____

Wall Color _____
- ☐ Flat ☐ Satin
- ☐ Matte ☐ Semi gloss
- ☐ Eggshell ☐ High gloss

Ceiling Color _____
- ☐ Flat ☐ Satin
- ☐ Matte ☐ Semi gloss
- ☐ Eggshell ☐ High gloss

Trim Color _____
- ☐ Flat ☐ Satin
- ☐ Matte ☐ Semi gloss
- ☐ Eggshell ☐ High gloss

Notes

Room Name _____

Wall Color _____
- ☐ Flat ☐ Satin
- ☐ Matte ☐ Semi gloss
- ☐ Eggshell ☐ High gloss

Ceiling Color _____
- ☐ Flat ☐ Satin
- ☐ Matte ☐ Semi gloss
- ☐ Eggshell ☐ High gloss

Trim Color _____
- ☐ Flat ☐ Satin
- ☐ Matte ☐ Semi gloss
- ☐ Eggshell ☐ High gloss

Notes

Date _____

Job Name _____ ph # _____

Job Address _____

Paint Brand _____

Room Name _____

Wall Color _____
- ☐ Flat ☐ Satin
- ☐ Matte ☐ Semi gloss
- ☐ Eggshell ☐ High gloss

Ceiling Color _____
- ☐ Flat ☐ Satin
- ☐ Matte ☐ Semi gloss
- ☐ Eggshell ☐ High gloss

Trim Color _____
- ☐ Flat ☐ Satin
- ☐ Matte ☐ Semi gloss
- ☐ Eggshell ☐ High gloss

Notes

Room Name _____

Wall Color _____
- ☐ Flat ☐ Satin
- ☐ Matte ☐ Semi gloss
- ☐ Eggshell ☐ High gloss

Ceiling Color _____
- ☐ Flat ☐ Satin
- ☐ Matte ☐ Semi gloss
- ☐ Eggshell ☐ High gloss

Trim Color _____
- ☐ Flat ☐ Satin
- ☐ Matte ☐ Semi gloss
- ☐ Eggshell ☐ High gloss

Notes

Date _____

Job Name _____ ph # _____

Job Address _____

Paint Brand _____

Room Name _____

Wall Color _____
- ☐ Flat ☐ Satin
- ☐ Matte ☐ Semi gloss
- ☐ Eggshell ☐ High gloss

Ceiling Color _____
- ☐ Flat ☐ Satin
- ☐ Matte ☐ Semi gloss
- ☐ Eggshell ☐ High gloss

Trim Color _____
- ☐ Flat ☐ Satin
- ☐ Matte ☐ Semi gloss
- ☐ Eggshell ☐ High gloss

Notes

Room Name _____

Wall Color _____
- ☐ Flat ☐ Satin
- ☐ Matte ☐ Semi gloss
- ☐ Eggshell ☐ High gloss

Ceiling Color _____
- ☐ Flat ☐ Satin
- ☐ Matte ☐ Semi gloss
- ☐ Eggshell ☐ High gloss

Trim Color _____
- ☐ Flat ☐ Satin
- ☐ Matte ☐ Semi gloss
- ☐ Eggshell ☐ High gloss

Notes

Date _____

Job Name _____ ph # _____

Job Address _____

Paint Brand _____

Room Name

☐ Flat	☐ Satin
☐ Matte	☐ Semi gloss
☐ Eggshell	☐ High gloss

Wall Color _____

☐ Flat	☐ Satin
☐ Matte	☐ Semi gloss
☐ Eggshell	☐ High gloss

Ceiling Color _____

☐ Flat	☐ Satin
☐ Matte	☐ Semi gloss
☐ Eggshell	☐ High gloss

Trim Color _____

Notes

Room Name

☐ Flat	☐ Satin
☐ Matte	☐ Semi gloss
☐ Eggshell	☐ High gloss

Wall Color _____

☐ Flat	☐ Satin
☐ Matte	☐ Semi gloss
☐ Eggshell	☐ High gloss

Ceiling Color _____

☐ Flat	☐ Satin
☐ Matte	☐ Semi gloss
☐ Eggshell	☐ High gloss

Trim Color _____

Notes

Date _____

Job Name _____   ph # _____

Job Address _____

Paint Brand _____

Room Name _____

Wall Color _____
- ☐ Flat ☐ Satin
- ☐ Matte ☐ Semi gloss
- ☐ Eggshell ☐ High gloss

Ceiling Color _____
- ☐ Flat ☐ Satin
- ☐ Matte ☐ Semi gloss
- ☐ Eggshell ☐ High gloss

Trim Color _____
- ☐ Flat ☐ Satin
- ☐ Matte ☐ Semi gloss
- ☐ Eggshell ☐ High gloss

Notes

Room Name _____

Wall Color _____
- ☐ Flat ☐ Satin
- ☐ Matte ☐ Semi gloss
- ☐ Eggshell ☐ High gloss

Ceiling Color _____
- ☐ Flat ☐ Satin
- ☐ Matte ☐ Semi gloss
- ☐ Eggshell ☐ High gloss

Trim Color _____
- ☐ Flat ☐ Satin
- ☐ Matte ☐ Semi gloss
- ☐ Eggshell ☐ High gloss

Notes

Date _____

Job Name _____ ph # _____

Job Address _____

Paint Brand _____

Room Name _____

Wall Color _____
- ☐ Flat ☐ Satin
- ☐ Matte ☐ Semi gloss
- ☐ Eggshell ☐ High gloss

Ceiling Color _____
- ☐ Flat ☐ Satin
- ☐ Matte ☐ Semi gloss
- ☐ Eggshell ☐ High gloss

Trim Color _____
- ☐ Flat ☐ Satin
- ☐ Matte ☐ Semi gloss
- ☐ Eggshell ☐ High gloss

Notes

Room Name _____

Wall Color _____
- ☐ Flat ☐ Satin
- ☐ Matte ☐ Semi gloss
- ☐ Eggshell ☐ High gloss

Ceiling Color _____
- ☐ Flat ☐ Satin
- ☐ Matte ☐ Semi gloss
- ☐ Eggshell ☐ High gloss

Trim Color _____
- ☐ Flat ☐ Satin
- ☐ Matte ☐ Semi gloss
- ☐ Eggshell ☐ High gloss

Notes

Date _____

Job Name _____ ph # _____

Job Address _____

Paint Brand _____

Room Name _____

Wall Color _____

☐ Flat	☐ Satin
☐ Matte	☐ Semi gloss
☐ Eggshell	☐ High gloss

Ceiling Color _____

☐ Flat	☐ Satin
☐ Matte	☐ Semi gloss
☐ Eggshell	☐ High gloss

Trim Color _____

☐ Flat	☐ Satin
☐ Matte	☐ Semi gloss
☐ Eggshell	☐ High gloss

Notes

Room Name _____

Wall Color _____

☐ Flat	☐ Satin
☐ Matte	☐ Semi gloss
☐ Eggshell	☐ High gloss

Ceiling Color _____

☐ Flat	☐ Satin
☐ Matte	☐ Semi gloss
☐ Eggshell	☐ High gloss

Trim Color _____

☐ Flat	☐ Satin
☐ Matte	☐ Semi gloss
☐ Eggshell	☐ High gloss

Notes